You Can Speak English but Can You Teach It?

By

Maud Robertson Ramsay Nomiyama

Strategic Book Publishing and Rights Co.

Strategic Book Publishing and Rights Co.
12620 FM 1960, Suite A4-507
Houston TX 77065
www.sbpra.com

ISBN: 978-1-62857-292-6

Dedication

To my daughter Lindsay Kawai M Ed in TESOL who specialized in bilingualism. She has worked alongside me for many years now and often brought me problems that she encountered for me to analyse and then we would both test the solutions.

Contents

Preface

Every child learns to speak his own language in two years. Why, then, does an adult, studying a foreign language, take so long to do the same thing? Is it because he has too many other things to study? Certainly not! No one has more things to learn than a newborn. For a baby, the whole world awaits. In two years, he learns to walk, to talk, to manipulate his body, to use tools . . . the list is endless. An adult achieving any one of these things in any given two years is justifiably proud of himself. Why do we lose this fantastic ability to learn so much, so completely, so quickly? The answer is that, actually, we do not—we simply subject ourselves to poorer teachers and poorer teaching methods as we become older.

Much has been written in the field of child development, and it is not the aim of this book to dabble in that field, but a quick look would help to answer our questions. D. C. Winnicot put forward the theory that "The Mother" was the best possible teacher that anyone could have. When one listens to his reasoned arguments and views the results of his research, it is hard to disagree. When one watches any mother, albeit the newest recruit, slowly, gently, carefully, and patiently guiding the baby step-by-step to the completion of his studies, one has to be impressed. No mother has ever been heard to offer the excuses that have been heard from professional teachers: "My student is not so bright." "I have no time to wait until he grasps the point." "He never takes clear notes." "He needs special tuition." "He does not listen to me."

After eight years of teaching, I returned to teacher training college in pursuit of better methods and devoured such books as Holt's *Why Children Fail* and Winnicot's *Child Development*. I became convinced that the best teacher was indeed the mother and that in order to teach better, one must study her ways. Bandura, Pavlov, Lorenz, et al reinforced these feelings in me, very strongly. Given any range of normality—and here I stress the word *any*—what mother ever failed to teach her child to walk, to talk, to eat, etc. within the two years that society allots to the task? Could I, as a professional teacher, equal or indeed better these standards?

I certainly tried. Never losing sight of my self-imposed task, I read, I tested, I taught, I travelled. I sought much. I gained much, especially during my world travels, when I was continually being confronted by different ways of thinking.

Japan was the epitome of this constant changing of ideas. In Japan, it is not the teacher who must continually strive to improve, but the student. For three years, I basked in the luxury of diligent pupils. I was lulled into a sense of complacency and smugness. But slowly, once again, the doubt crept in. Why was I, a professional who specialised in teaching (particularly teaching the very young), when given the world's most diligent students and often the most intelligent of these, still failing to achieve, far less beat, the record of a mother, any mother? Even extremely unintelligent mothers teaching extremely unintelligent children can have them speaking and walking within the two years. I, a sufficiently intelligent teacher, had been teaching doctors, dentists, and their ilk for three years. Why were they still unable to speak fluently?

I had to rethink my methods! I studied and read, read and studied. *The Psychology of Study* by E. C. Mace helped prise the blinkers from my eyes. As the blinkers fell away, I reread my previous books and realised that everything in them still rang true, but we were looking to the wrong teacher. My mind flashed back to when I had been lecturing in education. At that time, I had made a point of telling my students that there are five ways in which information can be channelled into the brain: by sight, by sound, by taste, by smell, and by touch. Mothers naturally teach at a highly efficient level. They kiss, they cuddle; they literally smother the baby with their love and their bodies. The baby SMELLS his mother's shampoo; FEELS her hair, her breath, her hands; SEES her lips and face; HEARS her voice; and quite literally TASTES his mother's skin. Teachers cannot hope to match that, but even with that caveat, they fall so very far short.

Most teachers are content to send even the most important pieces of information to their students through only two of nature's five ports: eyes and ears. I exhorted my students to do otherwise. A baby never learns at a rate of two out of five. Babies touch, smell, taste, look at, and listen to everything. Some of my students tested this and found that when introducing new material, remarkable results were achieved by stimulating more than two senses. Indeed, when five senses were stimulated, students tested two months later almost always showed a 100 percent retention rate.

With my past experiences in mind, I decided to examine the mother/child teaching/learning situation again. Further observation of mothers and children working together on a major project, such as walking, was startling in its revelation.

I slowly realised that the mother was not, after all, the perfect teacher. There was a better one: the child himself. Even all those years ago, it had been the child who had showed me that a teacher using only two of a student's five senses was teaching at a failure rate. Now I discovered that it was the child who had been showing the mother how to teach.

Being fresh to the job, she had responded naturally, following where the child led. As the mother/child relationship grew, the emphasis shifted, and the mother, anxious to do her best by the child, was no longer content simply to hold, to gaze, and to love the child, and follow where he led. She soon took over the lead and attempted to teach the child how to walk. To do so, she supported the baby from behind, pointing him in the direction she wished him to go and encouraging him to walk forwards—usually to the ever-obliging father, who would kneel down in front of the child to encourage the baby's forward progress. The child knew better. Babies walk sideways. The child is, indeed, father of the man.

I discovered this fact, which I now pass on to my students, teachers of English as a foreign language. Bearing all of this in mind and armed with my new insights, I carefully set about studying how exactly the child learned to speak his own language.

Who

If you are interested in reading this book, you are interested in teaching English as a foreign language. That means that you are either a non-native speaker who has attained a high English proficiency or you are a native speaker. Either way, you are perfect for the job.

Non-native Speaker – Same Base

If you are a non-native speaker who has mastered the intricacies of English well enough to teach it, and if you are teaching it to pupils whose mother tongue is that of your own, then you are perfect for the job. You will have the same base of thinking as your students. You will understand all of the difficulties involved in learning English, and you will have learned it from the same language base as your students. You will be able to guide pupils through the basics of learning English, and you will know the pitfalls that await students whose mother tongue is the same as your own.

Non-native Speaker – Different Base

If you are a non-native speaker who has mastered the intricacies of English well enough to teach it, and if you are teaching it to pupils whose mother tongue is not that of your own, then you are perfect for the job. You will understand all of the difficulties involved in learning English, and you will have learned it from another language base than your students, and so you will have three models of differing language rhythms. You will be able to guide your pupils through the basics of learning English, and you will know the pitfalls that await students whose rhythm base and pronunciation base differ from English. You will spot mistakes in pronunciation and rhythm more easily than same-language teachers.

Native Speaker

If you are a native speaker, you are totally perfect for the job. In fact, you are the most highly qualified person available.

If you are a native speaker, and you are more than ten years old, your qualifications are far, far higher than that of any university graduate. A university student gaining a master's degree need only attend university for five years. An adult native speaker has been using his language for twenty years or more—the equivalent of at least three such degrees.

If students of English merely want to be able to converse with foreigners and go sightseeing in foreign countries, they will need to converse with shopkeepers, hotel managers, and tour guides—all of whom are unlikely to have gone to university. It therefore makes no sense to prefer a teacher with a university degree. "Native speaker" is the highest qualification.

Many schools hiring people to teach English as a foreign language prefer teachers with university qualifications, and for these schools, there are some advantages to finding a teacher who has graduated from a university. Graduates will be more used to the school type of environment, will normally be more sedately dressed, and will often speak English with a more polished tone.

None of this adds to the qualification of being a native speaker. A native English speaker is the person needed for the job.

Graduate Native Speaker

EFL (English as a foreign language) students wishing to learn English so they can attend an English-speaking university will benefit from having a teacher with a university degree. They face, naturally, the problems of accents and slang speech. Most native speakers will know whether they themselves have heavy accents or not, and can try to guard against using very colloquial terms in the classroom.

In 2008, we invited many pipers and drummers to Japan to take part in "Pipefest Japan." There were people from Scotland, England, Ireland, Australia, Hong Kong, and Switzerland We had many Japanese volunteers who helped to lead the groups around the Kansai area of Japan. When the volunteers spoke to the participants, or vice versa, there were few problems, because the native speakers spoke politely and clearly, but when they held conversations between themselves the volunteers were almost always unable to follow completely. This happened even though the native speakers had no conscious intent to change their speech patterns.

I was checking up on how the volunteers were managing and asked if they had any questions or were having difficulties. One asked what she should do when any of the participants spoke Japanese and she was unable to understand. To the best of my knowledge, none of the participants spoke any Japanese, so I was very interested to know what had transpired. One of the young drummers had had a problem with his drum that was affecting the sound. He took it to his pipemajor, David Myles of the Forfar Pipeband and asked him for help. The older man fixed the drum, handed it to the young lad, and said, "Tak it awa an mak a rammy." The volunteers thought that the pipemajor was trying to speak Japanese. I explained that it was simply a Scottish accent and that he was actually saying, "Take it away and make a lot of noise." In the company of people from his own particular part of the country, he naturally lapsed into his native dialect, but just as naturally, when he spoke to people from other areas or other countries, he spoke in a clearer manner.

Many people who have heavy accents are aware of the fact and will alter their speech to suit the occasion. Indeed, there are often more problems with people who are unaware of their accents. I once asked an American teacher to arrive early for class and to make sure that during class he spoke clearly and, if possible, without much of an accent. "Sure," he replied. "Ah'll be there for twenny after nine an' ah'll speak nice and clear."

"Oh, so you will be in class for twenty past nine?" I said.

"Sure will. Twenny after nine suits me just fine."

When we talked about it later he said that he had recognized that I had an accent and that I had said twenty past nine. He had heard my accent but not his own.

Accents will always be a slight problem, but even with a modicum of English, the non-native speaker should be able to solicit clarity from any native speaker, regardless of accent.

A bigger problem than accents is the type of speech used by native speakers. Special attention needs to be paid to the age and gender of the teacher. In almost all languages, the speech of males tends to be coarser and more abrupt. Teachers should therefore be aware of this and guard against teaching students of the opposite gender words or phrases that are too coarse or too effeminate. Age, too, can be a problem. Would a young male student use the type of speech that his much older female teacher would use? I have heard quite offensive English from some young female students and found out in each case that the phrases had been used by her previous teacher, who was himself a non-native speaker.

This is why the native speaker is perfect for the job. When unsure of whether some English is gender related or age related, the native speaker can imagine it being spoken by his mother or his father, by his younger sister, by his brother, his teacher, or the local minister or priest. As a native speaker teaching your own language, you should always run every piece of English that you are about to teach through the "your mother/teacher/local pub" scenarios and check its suitability. Being able to do that is what makes you the expert. There is no higher qualification for teaching a language than being a native speaker.

However, according to the Japanese proverb, even monkeys fall from trees. Being an expert does not mean that you know everything. It does, however, mean that you are most likely able to spot something wrong. But what to do when you think or feel that something is wrong? That is when a linguist can help. There are many graduates who have studied the language; they can analyse what you have found and produce a name and probably a definition for it. There are many books written on the subject. However, these experts in language analysis are not necessarily experts in language acquisition. To be able to teach English as a second language, an expert in language acquisition is necessary.

Fortunately, such an expert is available for us all. This expert in language acquisition is, of course, the baby. Babies in every country all over the world learn their own language in two years. Some babies even manage quite a repertoire after only one year. Adults studying a foreign language often take ten years or more. It goes without saying, then, that to teach a language well, one must follow the route taken by the baby.

Every baby follows a clear route towards language acquisition. They do it at different speeds; some children dabble in the area ahead of their current level, and some regress to an area that they have already passed, but they all plod on through eight distinct levels. Sometimes, the levels overlap, but mainly they are very clear and separate. After one level has been mastered, the baby will move on to the next level, but will not abandon the previous level. More precisely, all language learning is akin to ascending a spiral staircase, with the student returning to the same area time and time again but at a higher level than before.

One of my favourite authors on the development of the baby is John Holt, who wrote several books, two of which I can highly recommend: *How Children Fail* and *How Children Learn*.

If she [Millicent Washburn Shin as quoted by Holt] were to find out that a thousand babies learned to stand at an average of forty-six weeks and two days, she would not know as much that is important about standing, as a stage in human progress, as she should have after watching a single baby carefully through the whole process. (*How Children Learn* by John Holt)

I heartily agree, and I advise teachers to study carefully any new baby and see for themselves how the baby learns to speak. In order to achieve success, teachers of language must follow this same pattern, in exactly the same order as the baby does. The eight steps that a baby travels on his route to linguistic success are: Listening, Pronunciation, Vocabulary, Rhythm, Speaking, Reading, Writing, and Grammar.

1) Listening - A newborn baby makes no attempt at speech for the first month or two. He only listens. He listens to natural rhythmic speech. He is not given simple, graded types of speech. He hears his language from the television and the radio, but mostly, in the beginning, he will hear his mother discussing many topics with visitors who call to see the newborn babe. John Hughes says that babies in understaffed foundling hospitals, who see very little of older people, are said to be almost silent, except for crying. (*How Children Learn* by John Holt)

2) Pronunciation - Soon the baby enters the second stage of learning. He works hard at pronunciation. He not only listens to the sounds made by those around him, but in his efforts to learn well, he investigates how these sounds are made. Anyone who has ever held a new baby who was learning to speak will attest to the fact that the child, not content to simply listen, wants to find out what is going on inside the mouth and will try to stick his fingers into the adult's mouth to explore the tongue actions.

3) Vocabulary - The baby now begins to amass quite a considerable vocabulary. However, no mother has ever given her baby ten new words to learn by tomorrow. In fact, in general, mothers do not give their babies any words to learn. Normally, a baby takes total responsibility for his own learning. If the mother or father wears glasses then the baby will surely learn the word for glasses. In short, vocabulary is chosen not dictated.

4) Rhythm - Now the baby drops all of his vocabulary and begins to talk gibberish. Many mothers panic when this happens, but, of course, these utterances are not truly gibberish. The clever child is experimenting with how his language sounds when it is all stuck together. "Ah no nonny nee nat" is a precursor for "I don't want to eat that." The baby is practicing his rhythm. Without rhythm, there can be no language.

5) Speaking - Having amassed a considerable vocabulary and then learned the pattern into which to slot these words, the baby now begins to speak, and he does so in many modes. He will use his new language ability to demand, wheedle, blame, fight, cajole, and report. He is now learning different ways of speaking.

6) Reading - Having learned how to speak at approximately two years old, the baby practices non-stop and so, three years later, he can chat away quite happily. He is a native speaker and, in Britain, he goes to school and learns how to read. In some English-speaking countries, children do

not start school until they are six years old, and so reading begins four years after speech has been learned and honed to perfection.

7) Writing - Having taught the child to read, the school now teaches him how to write. Such teaching comes in two parts. First, the child is given lessons in penmanship, and when he knows how to write the letters of the alphabet, when he can accurately reproduce the alphabet at will, the teacher moves on to how to use this new skill. The child is taught to write letters, reports, and stories.

8) Grammar - There are many aspects of grammar, and while some of them, such as spelling and dictation, are learned at the primary-school level, many more are withheld until the child moves up into secondary education levels. Grammar is therefore taught to children who have been using their English at native speaker level for more than ten years.

Many students of English as a foreign language are learning the language backwards. They are beginning with grammar, writing, and reading, and then cannot progress further. They become well and truly stuck at speaking. To follow in the steps of the baby, and where language learning is concerned there is no greater teacher, we must first help the students to spend a considerable amount of time listening to the language they wish to learn.

"All I am saying in this book can be summed up in two words: Trust Children" (*How Children Learn* by John Holt). We should heed his advice. If we accept that a baby learns to speak his own language in two years and that he spends the first three months making no sounds, then it follows that he has spent an eighth of that time simply listening.

Many books written on how to teach English deplore the amount of time that teachers spend talking to their students. "Bill Hull asks, 'Who needs the most practice talking in school? Who gets the most?'" (*How Children Learn* by John Holt). By this, of course, he was finding fault with teachers who talk too much to their classes. But how much is too much?

> Probably the single most important thing the language teacher can bear in mind as she stands in front of her class is that it is not her show. The tremendous amount of "teacher talk" produced by instructors who feel obliged to "perform" for the students and keep up non-stop patter lest the students start snoozing has been a problem since the Romans told their students how to learn Greek rather than letting them practice it themselves. The good teacher speaks in class only enough to get the students talking in the target language. (*Teaching Tactics for Japanese English Classrooms* by John Wharton)

By this, of course, he, too, was finding fault with teachers who talk too much to their classes. But again, we must ask ourselves: how much is too much? The baby will provide the answer. As shown previously, a baby spends approximately one-eighth of his time, before he begins to utter things, in simply listening. It follows, then, that as long as the teacher does not spend more than an eighth of the time allocated to her in speaking to the class, she cannot be faulted.

> Group work is especially good for managing a large
> class but should also be used liberally in any class since
> it reduces "teacher talk." Some Japanese students may
> think this is an unusual way to conduct a class since,
> in their minds, they came to work with a "gaijin," not
> listen to other Japanese speak broken English. (*Teaching
> Tactics for Japanese English Classrooms* by John Wharton)

It is, indeed, an unusual way to conduct a class and much
damage will be done by allowing students to listen to the
unnatural, arrhythmic speech of the other students. The
teacher, the native speaker, the expert, should speak as much
as possible, but no more than one eighth of the allotted time.
You, the teacher, are, after all, the expert.

Having found out who is qualified to teach and who the
expert is in this field it would now seem to be plain sailing.
The problem is, of course, that although the teacher can study
the baby to find out how he learned the language, the baby
cannot teach the teacher how to teach. Many native speakers
simply cannot teach. Teaching is a skill in its own right. In
order to help native English speakers teach their subject, we
started the Ramsay Method. This method of teaching gives the
native speaker a solid base in teaching techniques. There are
ten steps of achievement in the Ramsay Method, and anyone
who passes a level and receives a certificate for it will have a
worthwhile document to show prospective employers. Each
certificate shows what level the teacher has attained and fully
explains what the teacher can do, thereby helping employers
to judge how well that person can impart his or her knowledge
to students of English as a second language. "Suppose we
decided that we had to 'teach' children to speak. How would
we go about it?" (*How Children Learn* by John Holt).

Knowing what to teach and, most especially, how to go about it is fully covered in the ten levels of the Ramsay Method. The ten levels for teachers are:

Level 10: The teacher is able to train students to remain in control of what they hear

    a) by showing how to ask appropriate questions

    b) by showing how to extract clarity from a speaker with a heavy accent

Level 9: The teacher is able to train the students in the grammar of spoken English by showing how to compare it to that of written English

Level 8: The teacher is able to train the students in good penmanship and in the writing of imaginative prose

    a) by introducing the actions necessary for penmanship, in the correct order

    b) by showing that the power of English lies in the final part

Level 7: The teacher is able to train the students to read normal text, text contained within quotation marks, and text written in capital letters by referring the students back to the spoken English

Level 6: The teacher is able to train the students to enunciate standard formatted sentences

    a) by encouraging the students to ask for any items required

    b) by encouraging the students to volunteer information

Level 5: The teacher is able to train the students to recognize the power carried by a word depending on its position in the sentence

a) by helping the students to alter the rhythm to emphasise a word
b) by helping the students to enunciate numbers clearly and rhythmically

Level 4: The teacher is able to give the students a full understanding of a basic list of 750 words by helping the students to use their vocabulary to understand new words

Level 3: The teacher is able to help students eradicate any remnants of their own rhythm by showing how songs, poems, and chants distort the rhythm of a language

Level 2: The teacher is able to maximize the listening ability of the students

a) by captivating their interest
b) by moving the focus from large muscles to small muscles and then to theory

Level 1: The teacher is able to teach totally in English without recourse to the native language of the students

a) by constructing a well-balanced lesson with a clear aim
b) by introducing the aim clearly prior to teaching it
c) by showing clear means of consolidating what was taught
d) by testing, at the end of the lesson, that the aim was met

Teaching through these levels takes EFL students from total inability to fluency, and although all levels 1–10 can be used for adult classes, they should be used for any age. If fluency is required by the time the student finishes university, then levels 1 and 2 should be finished by the time the student finishes his nursery education, levels 3, 4, and 5 by the time he finishes primary school, levels 6 and 7 by the time he finishes junior high school, level 8 by the time he finishes senior secondary school, and levels 9 and 10 by the time he finishes university.

What

When you first go to teach, you will undoubtedly be looking for a textbook or a workbook you can use. This is as it should be, but remember: YOU ARE THE EXPERT. So often, I have seen teachers lose all vestige of common sense when confronted with text in a book. They view it as some sort of Holy Grail and do not use their own knowledge to judge the effectiveness or correctness of what they are trying to teach, relying only on the fact that *it is in the book*. Buy a book, by all means. Use the book to help you teach English. That is fair enough, but remember: YOU ARE THE EXPERT.

I have seen books—indeed, I have been given books by schools who wished me to teach from them—that were so bad, so far removed from English as to have almost been a foreign language, that I had to refuse to use them. I have taught English to non-native speakers in Scotland, New Zealand, Thailand, Korea, and Japan. In each and every one of these countries I was given books to use that contain utter rubbish and was assured that it was English. Even very highly qualified university graduates tried to convince me that it was English, only to be shocked when, three minutes later, I proved to them that what was written in the book is not fit to be used.

My first experience of this type of useless English was when I was in Thailand at a very elite school and was asked to teach English from a book that had been especially written for the school. The first lesson was, "My name is John Smith."

I gasped. "I cannot teach that!" I said.

"Why not?" asked the elegant English gentleman who was the head of the language department.

"The book is utter and complete rubbish," I told him, while I flicked through it to verify my thoughts and, to my horror, found more and more of the same.

I became aware of a lack of response, of a stillness, and looked up to see the gentleman's face contorted, bright red, and beginning to turn purple. "I wrote that book," he managed to spit out between his clenched teeth.

Not a good beginning, I thought to myself, but as defence comes very naturally to Scottish people, I simply handed him the book and said, "Then you show me how to teach from it."

"Couldn't be simpler," he grumped. "The first lesson is to teach the students how to tell people their name."

"Have the people that they are talking to been misbehaving or giving them a bad time in any way?" I asked. He stared at me as though I had grown horns. "Well," I continued, "I come from Glasgow, in Scotland, and I can assure you that if you go into a pub in Glasgow and say to someone, 'My name is John Smith,' you will be a very sorry person indeed, because someone will ask you just who you think you are and will then probably call to the barman that Mr. Important John Smith will stand a round of drinks for everyone in the pub." His face began to drain of colour. He began to realize exactly what I was saying, and had I been of a meeker and milder nature I would have left well alone. My point had been made. But by now the devil had me by the neck, and so

I continued driving the knife home. "Anyone who states, 'My name is John Smith,' is, at worst, declaring his superiority to all concerned, and at best, calling adoration to himself by claiming to be the person behind that world-famous name. Either way, it is a sure way to cause a fight. Hardly the correct way to start a conversation!"

"Oh, dear," he muttered. "I supposed we should say, "I am John Smith."

"Much of the same problem," I countered. "'I am' denotes a position, a superior position, as in, 'I am the class leader; I am the boss.' 'I am John Smith,' presupposes that John Smith is well known and holds a high position."

This is only one example of one book in one school. I have seen many such books in many such schools and in many countries. Remember: YOU ARE THE EXPERT.

When you see any English to be taught, imagine yourself in your local drinking establishment back home and try to imagine the reaction such foreign English would provoke. Remember: YOU ARE THE EXPERT. You can run the scenario over in your head several times. How would your mother react, how would your neighbour react, how would the teacher react, if you were to enter his class for the first time and say, "I am John Smith"?

I started out as a primary school teacher before lecturing in education at a technical college and then moving on to nursery education, and each and every student who entered any of my classes would wait until I asked their name or at least looked at them enquiringly before daring to introduce themselves, and even then, they would answer, "I'm John Smith." "My name is John Smith" would bring out retort from any teacher that I have ever known: "Okay, John Smith. You can sit at the back of the class until you learn how to speak to people."

Remember: YOU ARE THE EXPERT. Run everything through numerous scenarios and check if it invokes anger anywhere. The three main scenarios are in a bar, at home with your mother, and at school with your teacher. You are trying to teach your students to cope in a foreign land with foreigners. They do not need to learn how to provoke fights and yet most books teach fighting English. If you hear something that somehow just does not sound quite right, run it through the bar, mother, and teacher scenarios and test it out before you subject the students to it. Better still, run every single piece of English through these scenarios before you teach it.

Remember: YOU ARE THE NATIVE SPEAKER. YOU ARE THE EXPERT. As emphasized earlier, the native speaker must carefully assess any book that attempts to teach English as a foreign language. Many are totally unsuitable for use. This, however, does not allow the native speaker to simply teach anything he or she wants to teach. There is but one way to learn a language, and therefore it follows that there is only one way to teach it. Adults studying a foreign language often take ten years or more. All babies in all countries worldwide learn their own languages in two years. Some babies even manage quite a repertoire after only one year. To teach a language well, one must follow the route taken by the baby. The eight steps that a baby travels through on his route to linguistic success are Listening, Pronunciation, Vocabulary, Rhythm, Speaking, Reading, Writing, and Grammar.

Listening

Listening is a most important stage in the learning of a language. Never be tempted to teach English via the media of another language. To do so is to deprive the students of listening time—a most important time. John Holt tells of a French doctor who tried to teach a boy who had been reared by a pack of wolves how to talk. However, Victor, the wolf boy, never learned to speak. He had been deprived of the listening-to-language part of his education. "The problem wasn't that the doctor had given him more data than he could handle, but that he hadn't given him nearly enough" (*How Children Learn* by John Holt).

It is important to give students a fair amount of listening time at the start of each lesson. They have spent several days since their last lesson in listening to their own language. Following the pattern given to us by the baby, it behooves us to give the students, at the start of a sixty-minute lesson, ten minutes of simply listening to English. Always start a lesson by talking to the students. For teachers who are not confident about making up stories or jokes to catch the interest of the students each time, there are many wonderful texts available to read to the students to help them with their listening ability. Indeed, I have not come across any bad texts for listening. Do make sure that if you are reading to the students at the start of the lesson, you do so as smoothly and naturally as possible. The aim is to catch their interest and make them want to hear what is being said. For that reason, never choose an educational text or any other boring type of text. A clipping from a magazine or a newspaper would serve better.

Unfortunately, although there are many good texts for ensnaring the interest of students and helping them want to listen to what is being said, there are very few good listening *tests*. This lack is compounded by the fact that many schools want the listening ability of the students tested, so many otherwise worthwhile listening tests are ruined by a list of questions added at the end of the text. Adding questions changes everything, and so it no longer works as a listening test. There should never be questions after a listening test. Some teachers have protested that asking questions is the only way in which they can test whether a student has understood the passage or not. It is certainly not the only way—and it is assuredly the laziest way.

To prove it is a poor way to determine comprehension, we simply have to resort to our mother/teacher/bar scenario. I have no memory of my mother talking to me when I was a baby, but I have never heard a new mother questioning her new baby on the content of what she had just said. I can remember, very clearly, when I was a little older, hearing my mother say such things as, "Did you understand what I said?" However, she certainly was not testing my comprehension. She was warning me that I had better hurry up and do as she had said or I would be in very hot water. Had I answered her question with, "Yes. You told me to clear up my room and then dry the dishes," I would have been splattered across the living room walls, split down the middle into two equal parts—or, to be more honest, reduced to tears by a severe scolding, for my "cheek." I think that we can assume, then, that asking questions on text that has just been heard does not pass the "mother" scenario.

It does not pass the teacher scenario either. If the teacher asks if you have heard what she has just said, she, like the mother in the previous scenario, does not expect a repetition of her words. At best, she desires a simple, "Yes, miss."

Trying to run it through a bar scenario defies description. Most people prattling on in a bar can hardly remember what they themselves said. Expecting anyone else to even listen to them, far less to remember what they said, is beyond their expectations. All they really require is a nod of the head or some other action that tells them that it is acceptable to go on talking.

Indeed, in all three scenarios, answers are not expected. Actions are desired—actions ranging from an immediate jump up and run, to a polite bending to authority with a nod of the head, or a wave of the hand are the correct answers. In all three scenarios, if any speech is used, it is best kept to a minimum. "She [a seven- or eight-month-old baby] understood the game and when I said 'Bump,' she would bump her forehead against mine—and then give me a huge smile" (*How Children Learn* by John Holt).

It stands to reason, then, that any listening test should result in an action. In a school test, this seems, a first glance, to be an impossible task, but it is very easy. Instead of being given a paper full of questions to answer, the students should be given a blank sheet of paper and told to draw something on it, or they should be given a paper containing a maze or a map and told to follow the directions to find their way to a certain point. This would be a real listening test.

I remember once sitting in on a mock test, which I have tried to reconstruct to the best of my memory. We were told that it was a listening test to see if we could follow instructions. On the day of the test, we were all told to sit at our desks. The teacher laid out the test papers face-down on our desks. She strode to the front of the class and began. "Before you turn over the paper, let me run a few points past you. First, do not look at anyone else's paper. Second, when you finish the test or have decided that you can do no more, you will be free to leave the room. If you do so, please leave quietly, and put your paper on my desk before you leave.

Now, we are about to start the test. Make sure you read all the questions to the end of the test before you answer any of them. Start!"

We turned over our papers and there was the usual place for your name, the date, and your class. Below that, there was a large blank square followed by twenty instructions:

1) Draw a cross in the bottom right-hand corner of the square.

2) Draw a line going upwards from the cross until halfway up the box.

3) In the centre of the box, draw a small circle inside a larger one.

4) Draw a tree inside a triangle in the top left-hand corner.

5) . . .

Instructions five to nineteen were more of the same, becoming increasingly more complicated. The last one was a cracker, and although I sat through this test many, many years ago, it still makes me smile to think about it:

20) Now that you have come to the end of the instructions, it is important that you do not smile or laugh. Once you have read the instructions above, fold the paper in half, put it on my desk, and then leave the room. Do not write anything on the paper other than your own name.

We had been told that it was a listening test, and at the start of the test, the teacher had told us to read all the questions through to the end before we began the test. Few of us passed the test.

Although this was a fun test to teach us to listen well, the questions in this test could be used, if the instructions were given orally, to test listening comprehension. The EFL students would listen to someone speak while trying to glean some meaning from it. They could use that meaning as instructions to write or draw on paper so that their teacher could check if they had understood what they had been told to do.

Listening is an important part of learning a language, and so it stands to reason that it should be tested. Teachers, knowing the value of good listening ability, strive to give carefully selected, graded passages with questions at the end for the students to listen to and then answer. This seems sensible to them, but when one compares it to what the best teacher of the best student does, the lack of sense in it becomes apparent. The best student of a language is, of course, the baby—and so the mother can be assumed to be, if not the best teacher, at least a good one. A mother never gives her baby selected, graded material to listen to, and she NEVER questions him on what he has heard.

In order to establish what a good test of listening ability would be, we must first define "good listening ability." Good listening ability is NOT the ability to remember every word that was spoken. Even native speakers, after hearing a passage several times, find it impossible to remember everything. Indeed, it could be said that a good listening ability is the ability to ignore or forget most of what was heard. "There is typically a fair amount of redundancy in spoken language: people are likely to paraphrase what they have already said ('What I mean to say is . . . .'), and to remove this redundancy is to make the listening task unnatural" (*Testing for Language Teachers* by Arthur Hughes). We must guard against doing that. Native English speakers are so used to this redundancy that they automatically filter it out while listening. This ability of the native speaker to disregard unnecessary embellishments, to disregard rhetoric questions and to respond to only what is necessary is inbred. Even with all the good intentions in the world, no native speaker is able to repeat verbatim what he has heard.

If the listener does not have to perform any action as a result of what he is hearing and if the subject does not interest him, he will simply turn a deaf ear to what is being said and just politely nod every once in a while. To verify this just ask a policeman. Any policeman in any country will confirm the fact that if there are five eyewitnesses to a car accident in the middle of the day in broad daylight, all five witnesses will not agree on the colour of the car. If the policeman tests listening ability, the results are even worse. If he questions five people, five native speakers, on what they heard, he is unlikely to obtain agreement from any two people. This is guaranteed if the witnesses are given more than two or three sentences.

Give a full passage orally—a passage with the ubiquitous questions, such as I have often seen administered in schools—to any five native speakers and most of them will not score higher than fifty percent. It follows, then, that many schools are running listening tests that do not actually test listening ability. The type of listening test often given merely tests good behaviour, docility, and mostly unintelligence. Normally the more intelligent the student, the less he will want to sit and listen to artificial, arrhythmic, unnatural, stilted English.

To compound the problem, many of the questions have been made up by teachers who were READING the passage.

This method cannot and should not be used to test listening ability.

> We should avoid passages originally intended for reading, like the following, which appeared as an example of a listening comprehension passage for a well-known test: "She found herself in a corridor which was unfamiliar, but after trying one or two doors discovered her way back to the stone-flagged hall which opened onto the balcony. She listened for sounds of pursuit but heard none. The hall was spacious, devoid of decoration: no flowers, no pictures." (*Testing for Language Teachers* by Arthur Hughes)

I stress this point repeatedly in the teacher training classes that I run for teachers who teach English. Some of the teachers are native speakers, but most are not. As well as teaching them what to do, I encourage them to share any problems that they have encountered. One student teacher asked me about listening tests; she had one such test available. It was a passage about fairies and had five questions attached to it. Rather than preach to her about the rights and wrongs of it, I invited her to give the specially graded test to my nursery school pupils. These pupils are bilingual. They are taught daily in English and only in English. They play with each other in English and they also fight with each other in English. All of them failed. They failed because they were not interested. Some children would have passed had the test been about Pooh and some would have passed had it been about Pocket Monsters, but none passed a test on fairies.

25

Another student teacher showed me a listening test and one of the questions from the test. All but one of her students had failed to answer the question correctly and the one student who had answered the question was by no means one of her best students. The passage: *When he opened the door, the wizard who was wearing a long green robe and a long wavy, silky beard that was so long that it had to be tucked into his belt lest he trod on it and fell over, totally and completely blocked the opening.* The question: *What colour was the wizard's robe?* If the passage is read fluently and correctly, the word *green* will not be heard. It is in a clause in a long sentence and carries a very unimportant piece of information added not to impart information but to lend length to the passage, thereby improving the rhythm by giving the native speaker unimportant background noise in order to emphasize the blocking of the door. A native speaker would probably not even hear the word *green*.

To find out how to test listening ability, I told the student teachers to look at how the children in our nursery school listen. In general, mothers enrolling their children in nurseries hope their children will make friends. Children, contrary to their mothers' wishes, join nurseries and immediately make enemies—and it is because of this, that in our nursery school, they quickly master English. In our school, scratching, kicking, biting, and hair pulling—any kind of laying on of hands—are forbidden. We view nails and teeth as weapons. Use of either brings about immediate expulsion. Any other laying on of hands, or feet or whatever, results in a warning to the parents; expulsion follows if there is a further attack. Ergo, the children soon become masters of English in order to fight with each other.

Babies who have been allowed virtual freedom at home are, when they first arrive at the nursery, suddenly and firmly refused access to the toys they covet and are not allowed to play with them whenever and wherever they want. This very effective and strict policing of the nursery is sometimes done by the teachers but mostly by the other children. The children are much stricter than any adult. The other children, especially the older ones, are tyrants. Because we forbid any fighting—we even forbid physically stopping a child by grabbing him—the tyrants of the nursery (i.e. all of the other children) quickly become excellent at telling the child what not to do, graphically describing what will happen to him if he continues, and clearly and effectively taking his case to the teacher in charge should the culprit not desist. All the time the culprit is listening intently. He does not understand all of it, if any of it. He will not be questioned on his ability to understand what was said, but he "gets the gist." He is in trouble. This is verified for him by the look on the teacher's face as she approaches him.

Verification of a person's thoughts is an excellent way to teach. Indeed, it is the only way to teach. Success breeds success. Success smells sweet. Failure stinks! Yet, so many teachers teach failure. They do this by asking questions. Teachers in our nursery are not allowed to ask questions. The reason for this is because a child who answers a question correctly is lauded, yet a child who knew the answer but did not offer it for whatever reason is treated as a failure, often belittled, even vilified. This is unfair *and* it is bad teaching.

"The anxiety children feel at constantly being tested, their fear of failure, punishment, and disgrace, severely reduces their ability both to perceive and remember" (*How Children*

27

Fail by John Holt). "Dumb questions not only insult and anger children but often confuse them enough to destroy what they have already learned" (*How Children Learn* by John Holt). A child who knows the answer to a question but does not offer it refrains for many reasons. Often he is unsure because some idiot whispered the wrong answer, causing the child to doubt his own answer. He may think that his own answer is the better answer, but he does not want to offend his friend by rejecting the answer that was offered. His gallantry results in him being treated as a failure. A child who does not know the answer but manages to pull the correct answer out of the air or from the mouth of the child behind him is glorified.

Questioning students on what they have learned seldom produces good results. Questioning them on what they have heard is a test of confidence, luck, docility, or some other attribute, but it is not a test of listening ability.

The following example, which is taken from the ARELS examination, is one of a series of related tasks in which the candidate "visits" a friend who has been involved in a motor accident. The friend has hurt his hand, and the candidate (listening to a tape-recording) has to help Tom write his report of the accident. Time allowed for each piece of writing is indicated.

In this question you must write your answers. Tom also has to draw a sketch map of the accident. He has drawn the streets, but he can't write in the names. He asks you to fill in the details. Look at the sketch map in your book. Listen to Tom and write on the map what he tells you.

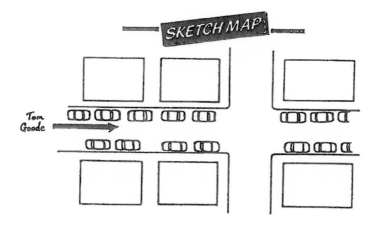

Tom: This is a rough map of where the accident happened. There's the main road going across with the cars parked on both sides of it – that's Queen St. You'd better write the name on it. – Queen St. (*five seconds*) And the smaller road going across it is called Green Road. Write Green Road on the smaller road. (*five seconds*) Now, I was riding along Queen St where the arrow is and the little boy ran into the road from my right, from between the two buildings on the right. The building on the corner is the Star Cinema – just write Star on the corner building. (*five seconds*) And the one next to it is the Post Office. Write P.O. on that building next to the cinema. (*five seconds*) Well the boy ran out between those two buildings, and into the road. Can you put an arrow in where the boy came from, like I did for me and the bike, but for the boy? (*five seconds*) When he ran out I turned left away from him and hit one of the parked cars. It was the second car back from the crossroads on the left. Put a cross on the second car back. (*three seconds*) It

29

was quite funny really. It was parked right outside the police station. A policeman heard the bang and came out at once. You'd better write Police on the police station there on the corner. (*five seconds*) I think that's all we need. Thanks very much. (*Testing for Language Teachers* by Arthur Hughes)

We must always check our definition of "good listening ability" before we make a test for listening. The more the students enjoy doing the tests, the better they will become. Games are a good way to provide enjoyment while ensuring that the students listen carefully. "Curious George at the Zoo" is one of the best examples of this. The game has a board showing the layout of the zoo with some cards and a spinner. There is also a handheld speaker. When the children press the button, they hear a voice with an American accent telling them of a problem which must be fixed before the busload of visitors arrives at the zoo. Even adults concentrate on what is being said so that they can play the game.

It cannot be stressed too often that good listening ability is not an ability to hear and to remember everything that was said. Good listening ability is the ability to disregard, to not even hear, anything that is irrelevant or uninteresting while at the same time managing to sift everything through a mental sieve to trap and retain only that which is relevant. This ability can be honed to perfection when the student studies the rhythm of the language and learns how to apply that knowledge—when he is learning *how* to sift through all that he hears.

"If recordings are made especially for the test then care must be taken to make them as natural as possible" (*Testing for Language Teachers* by Arthur Hughes). This would mean leaving in coughs and splutters, phrases such as "what I meant was . . . ," etc. But all too often, these very precious parts are edited out by well-meaning technicians.

When trying to listen to English, students must always pay particular attention to the final word. It is a very important word. "Danny (almost three) will often repeat the last word or two as if for practice" (*How Children Learn* by John Holt). It may seem as if Danny is repeating the last word or two for practice, but Danny knows that that is where the meaning lies. Danny has mastered most of the steps in acquiring his language and is now checking on the main point of rhythm, which is to highlight the important aspects of speech. Lessons on rhythm are imperative, as it is on these lessons that Speaking and Reading are based.

Pronunciation

Before teachers can embark on rhythm lessons, it is essential to teach pronunciation. Native speakers with differing accents often refrain from teaching pronunciation as they assume that their accent will hamper or interfere with it in some way. This is not the case. Pronunciation is essential, but although good enunciation is desired in the non-native speaker, many native speakers do not seek it. They prefer their own heavily-accented, slurred words to clearer, well-enunciated speech. Although heavily slurred accents lead to incomprehensible speech and should therefore be curbed in the interests of clarity, there is something romantic and attractive about accents. But they are not for the non-native speaker.

Clear speech may vary greatly with each individual accent but pronunciation is the same for everyone. Accents vary mostly on vowel sounds, whereas pronunciation focuses on consonants. An Englishman may ask a young girl to dance with him and the American may ask her to "daence." The Australian may well request a "deance" and a Scotsman would want to "daance." The Frenchman, being a non-native English speaker would probably ask the girl to "dince wiz im." None of it matters. The girl will get the message and the young man will get a partner. In fact, despite his pronunciation being the worst—or because of his pronunciation being the worst—the Frenchman will probably stand the best chance. Accents are interesting.

Vowel sounds can vary from greatly, from the short, clipped Englishman's vowels to the long, drawled, drawn-out vowels of the Scotsman. These differing vowels seldom pose a problem. Vowels are long or short depending on the accent of the teacher, and yet I have often heard teachers refer to long and short vowels when they wish to differentiate between the sound of the "a" in the word *bah* and the sound of the "a" in the word *bare*. This is not a good idea. Accents should not be taught, and teachers should not assume that their own accent is the correct one. In Scotland, the word *mat* has a longer vowel sound than the word *mate*. In England, the vowel sounds in both words are more or less equal, whereas in Australia and America, the opposite is often true.

No one hears his own accent clearly. This is natural, but what amazes me is that native English speakers can make some very wrong assumptions about the accents of others. "British pronounce the vowels in bath and bother similarly" (*Teaching Tactics for Japanese English Classrooms* by John Wharton). I am British, and I certainly do not pronounce these two words alike. Not only that, but I would not dare make any assumption about British accents. In Britain, accents can vary enormously from town to town. I have travelled across America from west to east by bus, I have travelled across Canada from west to east by train, and I have travelled across Australia in a figure of eight route from west to east by bus, and in all three countries, I was amazed at the similarity in accents within each of these countries. There were subtle differences but I could understand everyone. Not so in my own country.

I once gave a demonstration lesson in a town which was less than one hour's drive away from my house. Finishing a few minutes too early, I told the students to take out their reading books so that we could spend the last twenty minutes in practice for the following day. One little boy came up to speak to me: "Sez yow to ow is teem bit sez ow to yow is tintytyfowr." I could not understand him. Later, I found out that he was apparently trying to tell me that I had thought that we had still some time left, but that, in fact, it was twenty to four, and that the school would finish very shortly so there would be no time for us to practice reading.

Even in my own hometown, the local accent could be difficult. As a rule, the children were not allowed to use the Glasgow accent in schools and so when one little boy forgot and shouted out, "Haw miss! Kin ah go an get ma jaikit?" I politely reminded him that he should not use that accent in class. Soliciting the word *jacket* instead of *jaikit,* I simply said, "What is it called?" He replied with, "Aye miss. It's really freezin." Accents can cause problems, but they are also very attractive. It is quite amazing that in a country as small as Scotland, with a population of under six million people, the accents are so many and so varied.

No matter what accent the native speaker uses she is still the expert in her own language. She can still teach pronunciation, but care must be taken to ensure that her own accent is not being inadvertently taught to the students.

Where accents are concerned, vowels, as we have seen, are the main problem. Fortunately, they can be taught quickly, easily, and efficiently. Consonants are a bigger problem. It is therefore better to deal with the smaller problem first: the vowels.

Most Japanese students have an excellent grasp of music, and so they master the vowels sounds very easily when the sounds are matched to the solfa scale. I discovered this interesting fact because, being a very poor singer, I had great difficulty in Thailand trying to learn how to control the pitch of Thai vowels. I never did learn. To this day I cannot say the word for five (*hah*) in Thai. It needs to be sung very high, and I cannot reach it. In Thailand, if I needed to buy five of anything, I had to buy three items and then ask for another two. English is simpler for me but perhaps not for Thais, Chinese, or other high-pitched speakers. In English the vowel with the lowest pitch is "u" and the vowel with the highest pitch is "i". The "a," the "o," and the "e" are all roughly about the same pitch and can vary widely depending on accent. In Japan, the most difficult vowel for the students is the "i" and so it requires the most teaching.

When the teacher wishes to focus on vowels, a good pronunciation lesson involves giving students the following list and asking them to read one word from each of the pairs while the rest of the students circle which word they heard. At the same time, it is good for Listening, Vocabulary, Reading, and Spelling. It is also good fun.

Table #1

bid / bead,	biff / beef,	bin / bean,	blip / bleep,	bit/ beet
did / deed,	dill / deal,	dim / deem,	din / dean,	dip / deep
fill / feel,	fir / fear,	fit / feet,	gin / gene,	hid / heed
hill / heel,	hip / heap,	hit / heat,	jip / jeep,	kick / keek
kill / keel,	kin / keen,	kip / keep,	lid / lead,	lick / leek
lip / leap,	list / least,	mid / mead,	Mick / meek,	mill / meal
mitt / meat,	nil / kneel,	nip / neap,	nit / neat,	pick / peek
pill / peel,	pip / peep,	pit / peat,	rid / read,	riff / reef
rick / reek,	rill / reel,	rim / ream,	rip / reap,	Sid / seed
sick / seek,	sill / seal,	Sim / seam,	sin / seen,	sip / seep
sir / sere,	sit / seat,	tick / teak,	till / teal,	Tim / team
tin / teen,	tit / teat,	wick / week,	will / weal,	win / wean

In this way, vowels are easily taught and easily learned. An added bonus is that the students can see for themselves why they need to master the correct sound. A similar list can be made to help the students who confuse the "l" and "r" consonants.

In every language, when the baby isolates sounds and the pitch required to produce those sounds, it can be said that he is mastering the "vowels" of his language. "In France some years ago I was surprised to hear an eighteen month old boy, while babbling away, make the sound of the French 'u.' Perhaps there was no reason to be surprised; everyone who talked to him called him 'tu'" (*How Children Learn* by John Holt).

Millicent Washburn Shinn actually captured the precise moment when a baby who had been making sounds (vowels) happened on an embellishment of the sound, a control of the sound—a consonant:

A few days later the baby showed surprise more plainly. She lay making cheerful little sounds, and suddenly, by some new combination of the vocal organs, a small, high crow came out—doubtless causing a most novel sensation in the little throat, not to speak of the odd sound. The baby fell silent instantly, and a ludicrous look of astonishment overspread her face. Here was not only evidence of the germs of memory, but also the appearance of a new emotion, that of genuine surprise. (*How Children Learn* by John Holt)

As always, we must look to the baby when we need advice on how to teach language—in this case, before teaching the pronunciation of consonants. Most babies are first spoken to when they are lying helpless in a cot or a pram. At such a time, the doting mothers often lean over the babies and say something such as, "Who's a pretty baby, then?" The infants have had their first lessons in pronunciation. When teaching teachers how to teach pronunciation, I tell them to hold their hand three inches from their mouth and say, "Who's a pretty baby then?" The force of the breath on the hand allows the teacher to imagine the blast in the face that the baby receives at such a time. He now knows that certain letters carry a powerful output of breath.

When the baby becomes bigger, he is often spoken to while being held in his mother's arms. In that position, he feels the vibrations from her body as she speaks, and, of course, he also has the opportunity to look inside her mouth to see what the tongue is doing. At such times, the baby tries to stick their fingers into the mother's mouth and up her nose as he learns what facial actions are required for speech. These situations should be exploited by the teacher. As a young teacher, I used both of these methods when teaching deaf children and blind children. In imitation of the mother blasting her baby's face with the expulsion of breath required to pronounce certain letters, I would ask the students to hold their hand in front of their mouth and feel the expulsion of their own breath. When a student had difficulty with a word, I spoke the word into his hand and then asked him to repeat it into his own hand. He was then able to compare the differing strengths in the blasts of breath. When teaching students who are neither deaf nor blind, I tell them to hold their own hands in front of their own mouths. Speaking into a mirror held an inch or so from the mouth and comparing the breath clouds left by a properly pronounced word with those left by a badly pronounced word will also help to solve the problem. The mirror can be held at different angles to find out exactly how the breath leaves the mouth.

In imitation of the mother holding her baby close to her chest while talking, thereby giving the baby the vibrations necessary to pronounce words, I often told my students to put their hands flat on the table. Then, when I spoke to them, I leant forward so that my body was touching the edge of the table. In this way, the vibrations from my speech travelled across the table and were picked up by the students. This is a useful tip for teaching small classes while seated around a table. Deaf children are experts at picking up these vibrations. Hearing English students are often not aware that they are picking up the vibrations, but the improvement in their pronunciation proves that they did.

With large classes of children or even small classes of adults, it is more difficult to use the leaning-on-the-table-to-send-vibrations-method. Then, it is best to use the alphabet to show how the consonants should be pronounced.

First, it is important that the students understand that consonants do not "say" anything. Indeed, it is good to hammer home to the students that consonants have no sound at all. The letter "b" does not say "bih." I have heard many, many, many teachers ask their students if they can find a word that begins with "bih." The answer is, of course, that they cannot, because there is no such thing as a letter which says "bih." The name of a letter should never be confused with its sound. The name of the letter "a" is "A" as in *gate* and the sound it makes is "ah" as in *bat*. In English, the sounds come from vowels, and only from vowels, so a consonant can have no sound until it is followed by a vowel such as "bah," "beh," "bih," "boh," or "buh." It cannot be repeated often enough that a consonant has NO sound. Prior to teaching deaf children, I subscribed to the theory that there were two types of consonants: voiced and unvoiced. Teaching these children taught me otherwise. With fingers on the larynx, a common position for teaching deaf children how to speak, I found, to my surprise, that none of the consonants vibrated the vocal chords. I therefore recommend that the categories voiced and unvoiced consonants be viewed as a technicality not suitable for non-native speakers. Consonants such as the "b" in the words above, rather than making a sound themselves, control the sound made by the vowel. They do this by some sort of action. Each consonant is, in fact, a code for a certain type of facial action. The base of the spoken word is that each vowel sound is held for a moment and then brought to an end by an action which effectively stops the sound. An "a" followed by an "m" tells the reader to shut off the sound by closing the mouth and putting the two lips together to form the "m." In this way, sounds in English are stopped and started by actions, i.e. consonants. The actions required are clearly shown by the consonants.

In order to help EFL students to understand the actions necessary for good pronunciation, I set out the different actions required and made them into a chart. Although this chart is useful for any EFL student, I made it for Japanese students of English. Japanese is a "noun" language. The Japanese want to know what is there, what it looks like, and what it is called. Their written language "kanji" shows little pictures of what can be seen. English is a "verb" language. We want to know who did what, where they did it, why they did it, when they did it, and how they did it. Our written language mirrors this need to know the actions that are required. Our alphabet is akin to the Japanese kanji in that each letter is a little picture, a code—showing not what can be seen, but rather the action required to be made when wishing to communicate this letter to others.

Japanese students have tremendous difficulty in distinguishing between "l" and "r," and so I decided to start there. Always mindful that a good teacher never asks students to do what she wants to do, but rather always goes to where the student is, I reasoned that I would have to start with their own alphabet. I showed them that their kanji alphabet, a noun language, showed what could be seen by drawing little pictures and that our alphabet, a verb language, was a kanji (a little picture) showing not what could be seen but the actions required to make the vowels into words. The following diagram shows the student how to make an "l" and an "r."

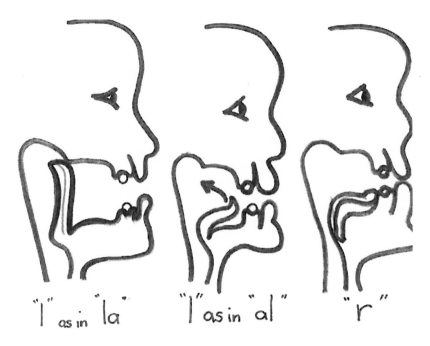

"l" as in "la"   "l" as in "al"   "r"

This viewpoint I then used to show the difference between "s" and "z."

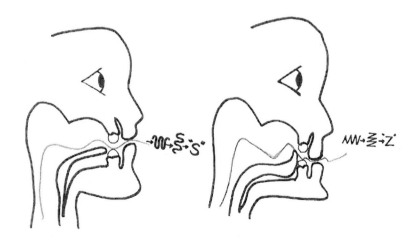

In the first picture the tongue, teeth, and lips are positioned in a way as to allow the air to flow over and under in an undulating fashion. In the second picture the tongue, teeth, and lips are held in a touching position to help vibrate the air as it passed over and under.

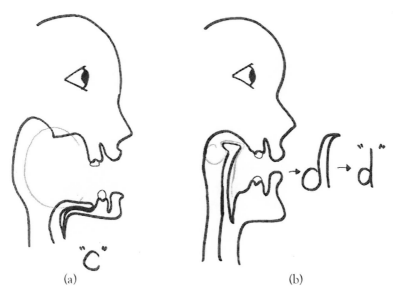

(a)   (b)

The next thing that I teach the students is that the mouth seen in this manner, from the side, is actually the base for many of our letters. This, of course, shows the action necessary for the letter "c." Here I use picture (b) to show that for the letter "d" we open the mouth, push the tongue up hard against the hard palate, and pull it down hard with a an explosion of breath. Here, again, it is helpful for any student who has difficulty, to compare the explosions of breath from the mouth of the teacher to that of his own. At this point, is good to hammer home the fact that consonants have no sound.

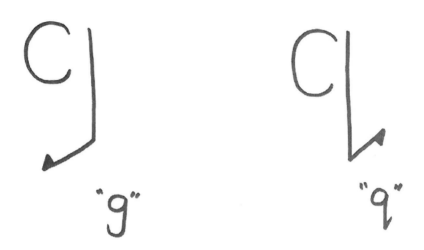

For the letter "g" we open the mouth and put the action down in the throat, but with a forward movement of the chin. For "q" we do the same, but with a backward movement.

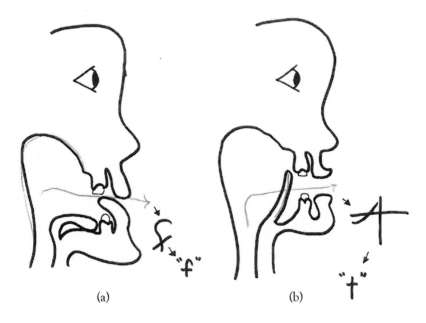

(a)   (b)

The next base movement for English is a stroke (a) signifying the breath being blown out of the mouth. We use it for the letter "f," whereby we hook the top teeth on top of the bottom lip, much like an umbrella hanging on a tabletop, and blow out. We also use it for the letter "t" (b). Here, the picture shows the tongue being lifted up to the top of the mouth and then blown down.

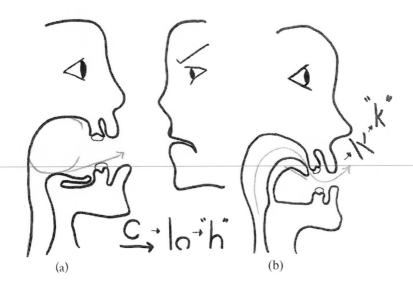

(a)   (b)

In the above diagram we have a composite of "mouth open" and "blow out." In (a) we see the two symbols used together showing the mouth open and the blowing out. As this is considered rude, it is adjusted to blow out slightly downwards. In (b) we see that the "k" uses the mouth open symbol with the blow out symbol and that the tongue should be held near the roof of the mouth for the cough. In fact "k" is often used with a "c" before it to emphasise this need for the mouth to be open. In (c) we see a similar action to the "k," but this time the tongue should move. Many native speakers do not necessarily move their mouths and their tongues as shown, but that is caused by regional dialects more than by any other reason.

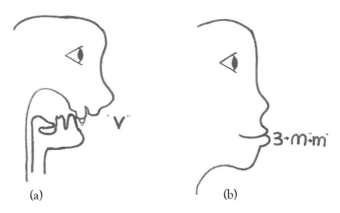

(a)   (b)

In (a) we see the mouth viewed from the side, with the importance of the overhang of the upper teeth being shown to perfection. In (b) the mouth is again seen from the side and the soft closure of the lips is seen clearly, but as this resembled the number three it was placed on its side and became the "m" as we know it.

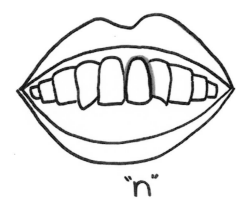

"n"

Here, the mouth is seen from the front and the importance of the teeth seen from this angle is obvious. In fact, it is part of our body language. The lifting of the front upper lip to expose the upper teeth is seen when the speaker is emphatically saying "No," and when seen without any speech attached, we take it as the speaker sending forth great negative vibes.

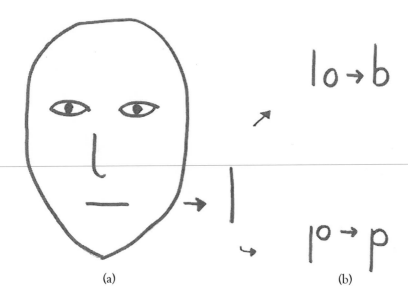

(a)   (b)

(a) Here again the mouth is seen from the front. The straight line symbol, in order to avoid confusion with the blow out symbol, was changed to a vertical stroke. The speaker is therefore required to close the mouth and make the action of blowing a bubble. In (b) the same actions are required but softer. It is interesting to note that this is used in music, too, to signify that the music marked thus should be played softly.

Here again the mouth is seen from the front. As the name implies—"double u"—the mouth should be placed in the position ready to make the "u" sound; then the position is released as a breath is taken, only to be placed that way again prior to sounding whatever vowel follows. Regardless of accent, there are few native speakers who do this anymore, but the non-native speaker instantly recognises the inhalation common to native speakers before making the sound of a vowel following the "w."

Many language professors have made great studies of our language, naming different kinds of consonants as belonging to different groups, and I bow to their knowledge. It must, however, be borne in mind that their studies have been made on the language after it has been learned. Having learned the language thoroughly, these graduates have scientifically analysed it. This is fine, but it often is of no use to the teacher who has no desire to know whether a consonant is a fricative, a plosive, an affricative, or a nasal, but who simply wishes to know how to teach it. In pushing these consonants into categories, many mistakes have been made.

–"Three of the letters are redundant (qc and x) since they duplicate k or ks" (*Teaching Tactics for Japanese English Classrooms* by John Wharton).

If they were redundant then we would have done away with them. The pronunciation charts above show how each letter is necessary and how each letter stipulates an action, its own action.

Vocabulary

Now that the baby can pronounce words, he begins to amass a considerable amount of them. It might seem "that since words are the shortest and simplest elements of the language, when we learn language we learn words first. But it is far more likely that we learn words last" (*How Children Learn* by John Holt). Vocabulary is by no means the first thing that a baby learns. First he has to listen and then he has to make sounds—sounds appropriate to his own language; i.e., pronunciation—but then he uses this same method of listening and making sounds to acquire vocabulary. As Holt says, he often learns the real words last.

I have two wonderful examples of that. My own daughter, prior to her second birthday, was at my mother's house where my father was watching television. "What's that?" she asked.

"Eh? Oh, sausages," said my father, looking at the plate of food on the screen.

For months after that she often asked for sausages for dinner. Being a cheap, simple, and very satisfying meal with little washing up afterwards, we often obliged, and then we all were able to sit down and watch television for quite some time before it was time for bed. It took almost two years for us to realize that she thought that the word for *television* was *sausages.*

The second example is one of many from our nursery school that sticks out above the rest. After they moved on from nursery to their Japanese primary schools, many of the pupils came back for Saturday school, where they studied normal school subjects in English. One day there was a jotter lying on the floor. "What is that?" I asked.

A student named Coco ran forward, picked up the jotter, looked at the cover and answered, "Sho Sho's Daddy!"

We had no one named Sho Sho. Our children were all Japanese, and Sho Sho sounded distinctly Chinese. "Who told you that?" I asked.

"Mrs. Kawai!" she answered most indignantly.

Mrs. Kawai, who was standing nearby, answered equally indignantly, "I did not!"

As they glared at each other, I rose and picked up the jotter. "Ah ha. Mrs. Kawai is indeed the culprit." The jotter was for "Social Studies." Coco would thereafter remember the words *social studies.* This is natural. The words that a baby learns are always chosen by himself. The mother, who is the baby's language teacher, never gives her student a list of words to learn by the next day or by the next week. The baby chooses his own words, and he chooses words that he will need in his own lifestyle.

"The things we learn because, for our own reasons, we really need to know them, we don't forget" (*How Children Learn* by John Holt). I would refine the comment above to make it read "the things we learn because, for our own reasons, we really want to learn them, we don't forget." In Japan, I belong to a group called the Association of Foreign

48

Wives of Japanese. Many of the foreign women who first join the group cannot speak Japanese. However, as soon as they go into hospital to have their first baby, their Japanese ability surges forward. They have discovered a strong desire to learn, and they learn only what suits them.

It is for this very reason that English must be taught in English. Teaching English by way of another language limits the amount of vocabulary that is offered to the students to only those words that the teacher has decided to teach. A new mother does not use another language to teach her baby English. A newborn baby cannot possibly understand the language that it hears shortly after birth, but yet, in two years, that same baby is able to speak his own language well. The baby is therefore telling us to use English and only English. The second reason for teaching English in English is that more time can be given to the learning of the language. Speaking in a foreign language during the lessons halves the amount of time given to the English language. It can therefore also be said to be dishonest to teach one language using another language to do so. At best the amount of time being dedicated to the chosen language, in our case English, is halved. If a student pays a teacher to teach English for one hour, the student has a right to expect to be taught English for one hour. He or she does not expect to hear that teacher talk in another language, especially in a language that he or she knows very well. "English classes should be taught in English" (*English Language Education in Japan,* Hideo Oka, July 2010). Teachers who teach English by way of another language often state that it is because the students would not understand what was being taught if they used only English. I have taught English in quite a few countries and have not been able to speak the language of that country. This posed no problem at all as I always taught English in English, and my students learned English quickly and well.

One of the main reasons for not teaching English by way of another language is that it deprives the students of much needed vocabulary. We must always remember that vocabulary is chosen by the student and not by the teacher. As a young teacher, I once taught a vocabulary lesson in which I wanted the students to learn the articles of clothing. After presenting each article of clothing, I used the word for it in a sentence. I wrote the word *skirt* on the blackboard and then told the students that the girl had worn a skirt to school. Next, I wrote the word *trousers* on the board and said that after school the girl had donned a pair of trousers. I continued in that manner with a number of items of clothing. It was no surprise to find out that some of the students had remembered some of the words and that a good number of words had been forgotten. It was a great surprise, however, to find out that all of the students had remembered the word *donned*. They had liked the word and so they remembered it. It was not one of the words that I had wanted them to learn, but it was English, and it was vocabulary, and it was good vocabulary.

How can one define good vocabulary? Vocabulary by definition is simply an array of words. Good vocabulary must, then, be an array of words that suit the individual. A pair of trousers is suitable vocabulary for a British person, but an American will refer to them as *pants*. If she can, the teacher should always tell her students if a word is different in America or Australia. However, it is better still to choose words which will not confuse. The word *trousers* is better than *pants,* because in Britain, *pants* will be interpreted as *underwear,* whereas in America, *trousers* will be understood. In Britain, we play football, but the Americans call the same game *soccer.* This time, the American version is better. Britons will understand *soccer* but Americans will confuse *football* with their own game, which Britons call American Football. However, none of the words will be a real problem, because all of them are nouns. Nouns are not ideal for inclusion in vocabulary lists. And yet, many vocabulary lists abound with them!

According to some sources a student should learn 750 words in the first year. This is a good amount, but more is better. To ensure that the student learns more than the required amount of words, the teacher should present many words to the student and allow the students to choose those which they want to learn. If the teacher requires her students to learn a list of ten words and she gives the students these ten words to learn, the result will be that approximately half of the class will not remember all ten words. However, if the students are given a list of thirty words and told to choose any ten to remember, the results are surprisingly better. A few students will have learned all thirty words. Some students will have learned much more than the ten words required and more than half of the students will have remembered the minimum of ten. I have tested this often, and the results are spectacular. Allowing the students to choose their vocabulary from a list prepared by the teacher ensures maximum retention and gives the students a feeling of enjoyment and power rather than that of forced study. Enjoying the lesson is one of the most important factors in ensuring maximum retention by students.

On the risers of the stairs leading up to the office from our nursery school, I have pasted on the following lines:

The teachers climb these stairs at night
The children stay below
Teachers building fires so bright
That children set aglow
Teaching brings the greatest joys
To all who would aspire
To help the children, girls or boys
To burn as bright as fire
But please remember when all is done
Did children, teachers, all have fun?

It is certainly not good poetry, but it is excellent advice. Make sure the students enjoy the lessons, and they will want more.

"The spirit behind such games should be a spirit of joy, foolishness, exuberance, like the spirit behind all good games, including the game of trying to find out how the world works, which we call education" (*How Children Learn* by John Holt). I'm afraid this is not what most people understand by the word *education*. They understand it as being made to go to a place called school, and there being made to learn something they don't much want to learn, under the threat that bad things will be done to them if they don't. Needless to say, most people don't much like this game, and stop playing as soon as they can (*How Children Learn* by John Holt).

Everyone knows that one must have fun, and yet few teachers follow through with it. It is amazing to think how often people exhort us to have fun in order to succeed. Mary Poppins tells us that a spoonful of sugar makes the medicine go down in the most delightful way. The dwarves in *Snow White* tell us to whistle while we work. In *The Sound of Music*, the governess achieves success with the children by helping them to enjoy their work as they learn to sing. Driving lessons home may produce good results in the short term, but kindling interest does much more. It builds for the future. There are many fun ways to teach vocabulary, and there are many good games on the market to help the teacher to do so. There are bingo games, board games, card games, and many more.

Many of them are good—but so, so many are not good at all. As a native speaker, you are the expert. Use your expertise to check all games and materials before you use them.

Most vocabulary games feature nouns. In Japan, almost all vocabulary books and games feature nouns. This is because Japanese is a noun language. They focus strongly on what they see. Their alphabet is composed of characters showing what can be seen. To compound the problem, many books written to teach vocabulary show pictures of items each labelled with a single word such as *skirt*. If there is no picture, then the word *skirt* can be written, but if there is a picture of a skirt, then the label should read "a skirt." Otherwise it leads the students to speak English while dropping the indefinite article. Sentences such as "Where is skirt?" are common, not only in Japan, but in many countries where I have taught English as a foreign language. The anomaly of these books is that when the word *shoe* is desired, the book often shows two shoes and the word *shoes* is written underneath. If pictures showing plural nouns have the label written in the plural, then pictures showing singular nouns need to have the label written in the singular. As the singular of *shoes* is *a shoe*, and the singular of *skirts* is *a skirt*, "a skirt" should be written. This would then help the students further when "a banana" is written under the picture of a banana but "an orange" under the picture of an orange.

Books on vocabulary rely heavily on nouns, but English is a verb language. Native English speakers do not want to know what can be seen.

One little Japanese boy who came to our nursery was continually being annoyed by a younger child who wanted to help him but was too young to do so. Every so often, we could hear Tatsuya telling Yoshino to go and play elsewhere. One day, she succeeded in gaining access to his Lego structure. He was furious. "Yoshino, you touch that again and you be dead," he yelled.

Before anyone could retaliate, I yelled out, "Tatsuya, come here." He came over very sullenly. "When you shouted at Yoshino just now, you were speaking English but you were thinking in Japanese. Japanese is a noun language so you told her what we would see; i.e. a dead body." He nodded, beginning to realize that that was indeed what he had thought. I continued, "English is a verb language. We do not say what we will see, we say what we will do. We say, 'If you touch that again I will kill you.'"

He was so happy and from that day on he used all of his English correctly in a verb format. Unfortunately, he went on to refine the lesson. One day, he yelled at Yoshino, "You touch that again and I will kill you like a slice of ham," graphically miming how he would do it. Once more, he was called to task for his bad language, but this time it was not the grammar that concerned me.

I have written a series of books for teaching English to very young children using vocabulary that is both meaningful and useful. The first book in the series, *My Doll*, has forty lessons. Ten lessons focus on the verb *to have*: "My doll has big, blue eyes." "My doll has long, curly hair." The next ten lessons are based on the verb *to wear*: "My doll wears a short, pink jacket." "My doll wears long, green ribbons." Lessons twenty-one to thirty are based on the verb *to like* but with positive and negative aspects of it: "My doll likes ice cream cones." "My doll doesn't like burnt toast." The final lessons are based on the negative aspect of several verbs: "My doll doesn't cry." "My doll doesn't shout."

A lot of vocabulary can be introduced by substituting items suggested by the children. They substitute things that they themselves like and dislike, and so the vocabulary is easily remembered. More importantly, it gives the students a pattern into which they can fit several other words. Most importantly, it features verbs, not nouns.

English speakers want to know who did what, where he did it, why he did it, how he did it, and when he did it. In English, we want to know all about the action. The fact that a man tore off his shirt in anger is more important than whether it was a shirt, a jumper, or a T-shirt. If we lack vocabulary but the word we need is a noun, then we have no problem. We can point to what we want or draw a picture of it, but without verbs, we are very lacking in our English language ability. If the non-native speaker gives the native speaker an approximation of a noun, the native speaker will soon be able to guess what was meant.

Riki Okamoto, a three-year-old child in our nursery, was having a hard time at the table one day. He wanted Hannah, an older child, to help him open his sweeties. She was willing to help him, but she was waiting for him to first say, "May I have this opened, please." He would not. Stubbornly, he tried sweetie after sweetie. Each time he looked up at Hannah with imploring eyes, but Hannah knew the rules. She was not about to lend her grown-up expertise to someone who would not ask for it. Try as he might, he could open none of them and was becoming more and more upset.

I was about to interfere and suggest that he try, "Help, please," but before I could do so, Riki suddenly turned to me with tears in his eyes and said, "Mrs. Ramsay, may I have a going-home-time, please?"

This was an excellent instance of verb material used to good advantage. When teaching vocabulary, is important to explain to students that in English we love verbs. We love them so much that many of our nouns are made from verbs. This can easily be seen in words such as *waiting room, departure lounge, chewing gum, diving board,* and *going-home-time.* This use of verbs to form nouns is easily seen in the previous words, but sometimes it is not so obvious. In words such as *table* and *desk,* it is more difficult. It needs to be pointed out that we eat at a table and we study at a desk. It is the use to which the item is put that decides which word should be used. Having a noun orientated language as their base, Japanese students like to *see* a difference in the items and so teachers often point out that a desk has drawers and a table does not. This method of teaching falls apart when the student sees a table with a cutlery drawer attached. We must remember to teach the students that it is the use, the action, the verb implicit in the noun, that determines its use.

Another example of this is the difference between a tennis court and a football pitch. They look similar. There is a difference in size, but if size is the criteria by which we choose then we would need to know how big a court has to be in order to be called a pitch. One look at the verb implicit in these words and all becomes clear. Thinking of the verbs *to court* and *to pitch* with their respective feelings of closeness and distance involved does more to help the students to understand which word to use rather than have them relying on images of size.

Words such as *this, that, these,* and *those* are often dealt with under the heading of grammar, but they, too, belong in the realm of vocabulary. They, too, have their base solidly stuck to a verb or an action. Students appreciate being told that if we touch something we use *this* and if we point to something we use *that*. Naturally, there are times when we do neither, but when we have to choose which word to use, thinking of the action implied makes it clear.

Consider "This is Mr. Jones." or "That is Mr. Jones." The latter has a nuance of rudeness attached to it, because it implies pointing a finger at the gentleman. If, however, the man is walking on the other side of the road, the idea of pointing a finger at him is correct for the speaker, for the listener, and even for the gentleman himself, were he to overhear. "This is Mr. Jones" conjures up a mental picture of laying one's open hand gently on the back of his shoulder. This makes the use of the word *this* quite correct.

All over the world, EFL teachers wish to give their students lists of vocabulary to learn, and naturally, these lists tend to be nouns. This will not change, and so I urge all teachers, when giving students nouns to learn, to group the nouns together according to their use and not according to some collective idea. In this way, a student who forgets a word can substitute another word which would give the same type of verb-like quality. Dishes, for example, are often grouped with *cups, saucers, plates,* etc. put together, whereas *cup, bowl, bucket, spoon, bath, Stetson* would be better grouped together as examples of items used to hold water for drinking purposes. Grouping nouns together in this way leads to fun lessons as students strive to find words to convey what is desired. They can use any of these words in a sentence, and although it may be totally wrong, the native speaker will be able to guess the message from the content of the sentence.

It also gives the student confidence to keep speaking instead of stopping and searching for the right word. Native speakers are never stuck for words when they are children. "Jackie (about two years old) . . . had created in his mind a class of objects that we would call 'dry, crumbly things to eat'—cookies, crackers, dry toast—to which he had given the name *Zee*. . . . When Tommy was about two, he met his first horses. One of them was named Duke, the other Blueberry . . . and from their names he invented his own word for horses in general—*dukeberries*" (*How Children Learn* by John Holt).

My sister Elizabeth, a native English speaker who has learned both French and German, when asked for advice regarding the learning of vocabulary for EFL students, simply said, "Don't chase the word!" This made us both laugh. When we were quite young, we had been on holiday together in France. Both of us knew French—she had studied French at university and I had picked it up after years of holidaying in France. But when we reached France, neither of us actually spoke any French. Both of us presumed that the other would be much more fluent, and neither of us wanted to speak French in front of the other, so we both continued to speak English. It was a ridiculous situation, but we were both rather embarrassed.

The situation remained unchanged until one day she lost her purse, and we had to report it to the police. She was very upset over the loss of the purse and so it fell to me to be the first to speak. We went to the police station, and I explained what had happened. During my explanation, the policeman was entranced by my daughter, who kept venturing towards him and then running back to me. He wanted to know what was wrong. I explained that in our country policemen do not wear guns and so she was mesmerized by the gun but also afraid of it. Another policeman joined in the conversation at this point and said, in a rather scathing tone, "But this is not true. I have been in your country and have seen policemen with guns."

I tried to explain that when a man has committed murder the police may arm themselves on that single occasion to hunt him down. I began, "*Quand an homme a fait la muer . . .* " but then I realized that I had forgotten the word for murder. Was it *la muerte, la muertier, la murdre*? I stuttered to a halt, chasing the word, and petered out halfway through the word itself. The policemen immediately fell about laughing. Stopping halfway through the word murder had made it sound like *l'amour*—French for love. "Ah, how brave are Scottish fathers!" he roared.

After that we both spoke French. The worst had happened and we had survived. Elizabeth emphasized that any word, even if it was not an approximation of the required word, would do, if it would help to keep the conversation going. I could not agree more. The native speaker is always able to seek clarity. There is nothing worse than trying to hold a conversation with someone who stops and thinks, and hems and haws until both speaker and listener become embarrassed.

So many teachers around the world give their EFL students lists of similar words to learn. Lists of colours and lists of numbers are common. The sad thing is that they are not needed. Students will always be able to remember their own favourite colour. For anything else, the three primary colours and the ability to use any two of them together will suffice. A bluish red, a bluish yellow, or a yellowish red plus the word "very" will cover any shade of colour that the student needs.

Children in their own language are often without vocabulary but they find ways of putting their meaning across. "Another of [Tommy's] early words was *down*. If he was being carried, 'Down,' meant 'Put me down,' and if he wasn't being carried, 'Down,' meant 'Pick me up.' His older sister, when she was very little, had invented a word, *tup-tup*, which meant exactly the same thing" (*How Children Learn* by John Holt). In another instance, Holt tells us that Tommy used the word *toe* to mean *toe, coat, cold, toilet* and *door*. "He may know the difference between a number of words, even if he cannot say the difference" (*How Children Learn* by John Holt).

This is true of adults, too. When I first came to Japan, I met a man whose name eluded me. To my ears it sounded like *sushi*. But everyone knows that sushi is raw fish laid on top of sweet, vinegared rice. Whenever I needed to say his name, I simply turned my head away and mumbled it. Eventually, I discerned a plosive sound before *sushi* and wondered if he was called *kushi*. But *kushi* is Japanese for *comb*. It surely could not be *kushi*. However, I sensed that he was better pleased with my efforts when I used *kushi* rather than *sushi*. Nonethless, I continued to mumble when I needed to say it. When he left, I asked my husband for the man's name. It was Atsushi. Now I never forget his name. I have learned it as a piece of sushi preceded by a sneeze.

Learning should be a pleasure. Yet so often teachers of English as a foreign language give their poor students lists of numbers, days of week, months of the year, etc., to remember. This is not teaching. It is cruelty. No one needs to know all of the days of the week, or all of the months of year, or all of the numbers.

Shortly after the end of the Second World War, I was sent out to the outer islands of Scotland, while my parents stayed in Glasgow. The people of South Uist spoke only Gaelic. English was seldom heard. I became fluent in Gaelic but I never bothered to learn the numbers because they were too difficult. This lack of numbers never once gave me a problem. Everyone will happily write out a number on a piece of paper or even on the palm of his hand using his finger as a pencil. Gaelic and French have a system of calling large numbers a compound of lesser numbers, so that *ninety* becomes *four-twenties-plus-ten.* Complications like that I can do without.

In Thailand, I had another type of complication with numbers. I could not sing the word *hah* at the correct pitch to signify the word *five,* so I found ways around it. In Burma, my seven-year-old daughter always bought seven articles even if we only needed three. The word for *seven* in Burmese is *shit,* and she simply loved to ask for seven bananas. She needed no other numbers.

I have visited forty-three countries, lived in at least eleven of them, and struggled with more than six languages. I could not afford to waste my time in learning lists of vocabulary such as days of the week or months of the year. I needed only to know the name for Monday and the name of the month in which I was born. By holding up my fingers and pointing to the first finger and calling it Monday, I could solicit the name for any other day of the week that I required. Similarly, by pointing to each finger in turn, I could name the finger corresponding to my month, which was November, and thereby solicit December. Starting again from the first finger, I found it easy to solicit the names of the months from the native speaker until I found the name for the month I needed. It would have been easier, of course, if I had been born in February or March.

Learning a list of words is not fun. Learning should be fun. A good and enjoyable way to teach vocabulary is to have students make a sentence and leave out a word; then all the other students guess what the word could be. Not only do the students enjoy this game, it produces many more words than the teacher would have thought to offer, and it shows the students that there is more than one possible answer. "Thus naming things is not just blind imitation; it is a creative act of the mind" (*How Children Learn* by John Holt).

Teachers must consider carefully the vocabulary that they give to students. The ability to describe people is essential, and yet it is a need that is not often addressed in the teaching of vocabulary. In an emergency, they may have a great need to describe someone, so this should be one of the first things students learn how to do. They need to know that with English being a verb language, when describing people, we start with the attributes that do not readily change and finish up with the items that can change on a daily basis. To fill this need, I devised a format for the students to use; it begins with the person's height and weight and pertinent facial features; moves on to hair length, colour, and style; and then finishes with the clothes worn by that person. The students all enjoy drawing figures for the other students to describe. Having pictures of five or six figures available for students to identify while another student delivers a description makes a very enjoyable lesson.

Rhythm

After the baby has amassed a goodly amount of vocabulary, he addresses the problem of stringing them all together. Now he is learning to sing the song that is his language.

"Sitting in his stroller in a local shop the other day was a child about a year old . . . Suddenly he said to himself 'Beng-goo.' . . . Was he trying to say, 'Thank you'? More probably, he had hit on this sound by accident and was saying it over and over because he liked the way it felt in his mouth" (*How Children Learn* by John Holt). Holt's observation is wonderful, but it is more likely that the baby was more interested in fitting "thank you" into its proper rhythm than clearly enunciating the word. "[A]nother one-year-old. . . . liked to say 'Leedle-leedle-leedle-leedle' (*How Children Learn* by John Holt). Again in this second example, which Holt attributes to pronunciation, it is more likely that the child is experimenting with rhythm. Had the child been repeating the word ad infinitum, it would certainly have been a case of the baby practicing pronunciation, but the fact that the baby said it four times and repeated this four-part pattern makes it clearly a case of rhythm practice.

When I first came to Japan, I spent a considerable amount of time as an itinerant teacher going from house to house to give private English lessons. Normally, the houses were large, and the entrance hall was quite a distance from the living room. The custom in Japan is to stand in the hallway just inside the door and shout, "O-jama-shima-su." This was difficult for me. However, I solved the problem by reasoning that if I could just find something that I could easily remember and force into the four-beat rhythm, it would pass muster. I reasoned that in my own country we would bring a cake or a bottle of wine when we visit, but this being Japan, it would fit my purposes to bring pyjamas in a little Japanese dish for serving rice; a *chawan*. This funny scenario was easily remembered, and so I would open the door, bow low, and shout "Oh, pyjamas in *chawans!*" Nobody ever found it strange. Every Japanese person heard "*O-jama-shima-su.*" Since then, I have heard people tell of similar situations. When one is thanked by a Japanese person, in Japanese the polite reply is "*doi-tashi-mash-itteh.*" The foreigner unable to remember this piece of Japanese simply says, "Don't touch my moustache."

In speaking any language, the rhythm is the most important part and yet many teachers ignore it altogether or worse still butcher it, often citing clear speech as the reason for ruining good rhythm.

"When Patrick . . . was just over two years old, he could not pronounce a Z, SH, CH or any other sibilant sounds. He just left them out. Words like *spoon* became 'poon'" (*How Children Learn* by John Holt). This is a perfect example of a child simply removing a difficulty in order to conserve the rhythm. Adult native speakers do this all the time. Sentences such as "It is not black" become "Snot black." Striving for good enunciation is admirable, but if a teacher does so at the expense of rhythm, much harm can be done.

What would have happened if we had dealt with [Patrick] as we deal with children in school? Instead of giving him time to correct his own speech, to grow competent and confident in making his sibilants, we would have been correcting him every time he spoke. "No, not 'poon,' 'spoon.' S-s-s-spoon. Say it, *spoon, spoon, spoon.*' We might have grown more impatient and angry, the child more discouraged and frightened. . . . Perhaps he might have decided to stop talking altogether. . . . Or he might have developed a stutter or a stammer; as Wendell Johnson and other speech therapists have pointed out, this is how stutters and stammers are made. (*How Children Learn* by John Holt)

Holt is treating this as an inability to pronounce certain sounds whereas I see it as the child simply handling a rhythm difficulty. I do not, however, take any issue at the point he has made regarding the handling of the problem. When working as a specialist teacher, I often had to help children who had developed a stutter. Having seen the anguish suffered by these children, I cannot condone anything that would induce a stutter. The problem is that we are paid to teach, and so we simply cannot wait until a child corrects his own mistakes, no matter how admirable that may be. To take money for teaching children and then to leave the child to correct himself smacks of dishonesty.

Besides, in my experience, children struggling with the rhythm of the language often drop any letter that is interfering with their ability to push the language into its proper rhythm. Simply helping these children with their rhythm by showing them what letters to throw away and what letters to keep tends to clear up these problems very quickly and gives no grief to the child. In everyday discourse, clear speech is rarely ever used. Many words are, quite correctly, contracted to almost oblivion. As teachers, we must choose wisely which words to correct and which to ignore.

My classes are always fascinated by the fact that when I hand over my ticket to the ticket collector at the station I never say "Thank you." I always say "Kyu." They have never realized that there was such a word as *kyu*, and yet when I ask them to listen for it, they all come back astonished at how often they hear it. Some even report hearing, "N kyu."

Speech, in order to comply with the rules of rhythm, is perforce squashed and stretched. Every native speaker does this and every English speaker must do it. Indeed, Americans have gone so far as to change *want to* into *wanna* and *going to* into *gonna*. The Australians have changed *good day* into *g'day*. These examples belong in the region of slang, but they do help to show the readiness with which squashed speech is used and accepted. Indeed, if speech is not squashed to fit the rhythm, the sense of the words is often lost.

A perfect example of that is when non-native speakers try to say, "I am going to town." Firstly, *I am* needs to be squashed into *I'm*, thereby becoming, "I'm going to town." This, however, is not enough. The *to* needs to be squashed until it becomes simply a "t"; otherwise, the native speaker hears "I'm going too . . .town" and has to struggle to pull some sense out of what he has just heard. The word *to* is always reduced to "t" in speech. This helps to fit it into the rhythm of the sentence, but it also helps to clarify the meaning and differentiate it from the word *too*.

There are three words in the English language which non-native speakers often pronounce as "too." They are *to*, *too*, and *two*. It is useful to remind the students how the two letters "oo" are pronounced. Then they should be told that the "w" in the word *two* tells the speaker to sound the vowel twice so that the word *two* becomes "too-oo." Many students of English have difficulty in understanding that *to*, *two*, and *too* are not only spelled differently but spoken differently, too. To help them understand this better, I made three sentences for them to read aloud:

He's going from small to big.
He's getting too big for his boots.
He's buying two big apples.

This helps them to understand why I cannot hear which word they are trying to use when they use it with the wrong rhythm.

The words *four* and *for* come under the same rule. Even when speaking clearly and with good enunciation, the word *for* is never clearly enounced. It is always contracted to "f'r." Over-enunciation distorts the meaning of the word, and the native speaker hears "four."

One other important rule to be followed when dealing with these little words is that in English, "the little words go on." A good example for this can be found in the sentence "Mary is going to learn how to drive so that she can go to town in her father's car." If the little words are not scrunched together, the rhythm is ruined and the meaning becomes difficult to grasp. As explained before, a pause after "Mary is going to" changes the meaning, and the listener hears "Mary is going as well." The words "is going to learn how to drive" need to be run together and to become "isgoingtolearnhowtodrive." Similarly "so that she can go to town" should be spoken as one word. Unfortunately for the Japanese who wish to speak English, their language is almost exactly the opposite of ours. In Japanese the small words go backwards and stick onto the important words that precede them. It is therefore very important to show Japanese speakers of English how to tie their English words together to comply with the rules of rhythm.

As this tends to be a difficult lesson for foreign students, I put the words "not at all" up on the blackboard and ask several students to read them. All of them, usually, read them "correctly." When I point out that none of them read what I had written I become the focus of their attention. Every student in the class is so sure that the sentence was read correctly as to be almost bored by whatever was coming next. To be told that no one read it correctly jolts them out of any complacent reverie that they might have begun.

I tell them that I wrote "Not at all" while pointing to each word quite slowly as I say it. At this point I stop speaking and write, "No ta tall." The lights begin to come on in the faces around me. "You were 'correct in reading' it as it should have been read, BUT you did not read what I had written. Now, it is important that you continue to use what you have just learned when you read or speak English. Remember, all the little words go on and all the final consonants go on."

In fact, if there is no final consonant then we just simply put one in. This confuses them and so a very pleasant time is had while the students read out the words that I write. "I wi lea ta banana, I will dry va car, I will pee la grape, I wi lea ta napple." It is no exaggeration to say that the class is now filled with interested faces as the students understand the sentences; these faces turn happy as the last sentence is written and they realize that the "n" has been gratuitously dropped into the sentence. This is what the teacher meant by the difference between *a* and *an*. This is why we say "an apple" and not simply "apple." Everyone, child or adult, likes to think that he worked things out for himself. Something that students discover for themselves is easily remembered.

"Children when they are making something as simple as a mud pie, want to make it as well as they can, not to please someone else but to satisfy themselves" (*How Children Learn* by John Holt).

Every language has rhythm, and every language has rules for the rhythm that it uses. English uses a three-beat rhythm. It is easier to teach this rhythm to the students if they understand the rhythm of their own language. Japanese uses a four-beat rhythm; once the students understand this, they find it easier to change to the three-beat rhythm of English.

English is based on three-letter words. The basic structure is a vowel sandwich—a consonant, a vowel, and then a consonant. Words such as *cat, dog,* and *pet* are examples of this. Three of these words put together form a nine-letter format found in words such as *badminton*. This "triple sandwich" is less common than a double-decker type of sandwich whereby two sandwiches are used to sandwich a vowel, as in *daff-o-dil, sell-o-tape* and *fan-a-tic*. In this type of word, the three-beat rhythm is nevertheless maintained, and so the centre vowel is held longer in order to give it the same length of time as the first and the last parts of the word.

This lengthening of the centre vowel is recognized by many teachers of English, but it is often mistakenly referred to as an accent. In Japan, I once saw a test in which the students were asked to mark each word in a list to show where the accent would fall. When I pointed out that had the question been worded in such a way as to ask where the stress should be it would have been better.

Without knowing what accent is being used, it is impossible to answer such a question. I pointed out to the teacher that I am British, and so my accent would make me stress the centre part of the word, but that an American would accentuate the first part of the word and an Australian would put the accent on the end of the word—i.e. **1**,2,3 for Americans, 1,**2**,3 for Britons, and 1,2,**3** for Australians. This seemed to puzzle the teacher, and so for her benefit,

I thought up the following examples. Although it was over thirty years ago, I still use them today.

The same sentence, 'He's an American from the United States of America', said as it were by each of the three different nationalities mentioned above would differ greatly. The word 'American' has four parts – A-mer-i-can. Seeking a three beat rhythm we tend to throw out the first part, the 'A'. The Americans then stress the first part so that it becomes **Mer**-i-can or even **Murr**-i-can, whereas the British stress the centre part thereby making it Mer-**iiii**-can. This rhythm is carried on in the last part of the sentence whereby the phrase 'United States of America' is stressed in the beginning by Americans, in the middle by Britons, and at the end by Australians.

Table #2

USA	–	He's an (A)-murr-i-can from the <u>United</u> States of America
UK	–	He's an (A)-mer-<u>iiii</u>-can from the United <u>States</u> of America
AUS	–	He's an (A)-mer-i-<u>caan</u> from the United States of <u>America</u>

Non-native speakers of English should not try to imitate these accents in any way. From them an unaccented three beats is best.

Non-native speaker – He's an American from the United States of America.

"Americans also customarily pronounce the unstressed syllables that Britons often drop such as 'lab'ratory' instead of the British 'laborat'ry'" (*Teaching Tactics for Japanese English Classrooms* by John Wharton). This is a good example of the natural rhythms of Americans and Britons. In English, every sentence and every word must fit into a three-beat rhythm, and a word such as *laboratory* poses a problem because it has more than three parts. With such a large word, some part needs to be scrunched into another part to make it fit the three-beat rule. The word *laboratory* therefore becomes "labo-ra-tory." Americans, having a **123** rhythm will naturally talk about a "**lab**-ora-tory," which is somewhat difficult to say and soon becomes "**lab**'ratory." Britons will talk about a "lab-**ora**-tory," which is also somewhat difficult to say and soon becomes "lab**orat**'ry."

From this it can be clearly seen that although the non-native speaker should not accentuate any part of the sentence, he will need to run some of the words and some parts of the words together while holding or stretching other parts, so that each part takes up the same amount of time.

One other area where the three-beat rhythm needs to be emphasized is numbers. Many non-native speakers are unable to differentiate between the numbers *thirteen* and *thirty*. This changes when they are shown that every number should follow a three-beat rhythm and that once double figures are reached, the units part of the number receives only one beat while the tens part of the number receives two beats. Following this rule, the word *thirty* becomes "thi-ir-ty" and *thirteen* becomes "thir-tee-een."

In Japanese, the numbering system is based on the position of the number. The Japanese think that each position has an importance and that each position has a name. They give importance to a figure, such as a 3, by considering whether it is in, say, the ones position or the millions position. It is very confusing when they try to use this system for English numbers. They are delighted to learn that our system is much easier than theirs.

Although at first glance it would appear to be the same, it is not. We do not name the positions in our numbering system. Most Japanese students try to read out large numbers based on the positions held by them as in the following table.

Table #3

Hundred millions	Ten millions	millions	Hundred thousands	Ten thousands	thousands	hundreds	tens	units

Students then try to read the number by trying to fit it into the appropriate box and apply the appropriate heading to it. Trying to remember the names of each position is an extremely difficult and onerous task. Most students—and indeed, even some teachers that I have taught—are very surprised to find that, in fact, our numbering system does not use these headings at all when reading out numbers. In English, numbers, when spoken, follow a much simpler formula. As stated previously, the positions are not named at all. Instead the position of the numbers is implied by the name given to the commas which divide the numbers.

Table #4

-	million	-	-	-	thousand	-	-	-

The first comma, naming them from right to left, is named *thousand* and the second comma is named *million*. A large number such as 123,456,789 is best explained by using three similar parts. When teaching notation, the use of a number with each part identical, such as 123,123,123, makes it easier for the students to understand that it is that only the names of the commas that need to be remembered. They are so happy to realize that no matter where the three numbers appear in the lineup, these numbers 123 read as "one hundred and twenty-three" and the immensity of the number is implied simply by naming the commas. The number becomes "one hundred and twenty-three **million**, one hundred and twenty-three **thousand**, one hundred and twenty-three."

There are many new and interesting ways to bring notation to students. Some ways are better than others, but once students understand the principle behind the naming of the commas, they enjoy writing down numbers read out by the teacher. Another variation, which is even more effective, is for the students to each read out a number for the rest of the class, including the teacher, to write down. Most of the students in the class do not remember who read out which number, but the student who read out a number that the teacher wrote wrongly inwardly cringes, and he knows that he must improve his number reading ability.

There are many songs and chants which feature numbers, and many teachers mistakenly think they will help students. Giving songs and chants to students to help them with number skills is not a good idea. Songs and chants are good for helping children to remember vocabulary, but they utterly destroy the rhythm of the language. If numbers are included in the song or poem, then the student is learning the number with the wrong rhythm and then this will have to be corrected later.

Poetry is poetry because it takes the natural rhythm of speech and pulls it and forces it into a new and predetermined format which is totally unnatural. It is interesting to note that English speakers take their natural three-beat rhythm and turn it into four beats when they make poetry. The Japanese speakers take their natural four-beat rhythm and turn into three beats when they make poetry. Singing songs with numbers in them is no problem for native speakers. They recognize that the rhythm has been distorted. Non-native speakers, not knowing this, are left with a strange arrhythmic type of speech. For this reason teachers must be careful not to give students, especially very young students, too many rhymes, songs, or chants.

When young children are given something accompanied with "Here you are," the automatic response of "Thank you" almost turns the two sentences into a chant. This is acceptable, but only if the natural rhythm is maintained. When there are only two words in a sentence, it is often hard for the non-native speaker to understand how to apply a three-beat rhythm to the two words. Another difficult point for them to understand is that the meaning of the sentence changes with a change in rhythm. A sentence such as "Thank you." needs two beats on one of the words. The normal inflexion is to give two beats to the first word so that it is uttered as "Tha-ank you." If the second word is given two beats, as in "Thank yo-ou," the meaning changes. This second type of rhythm is often used when someone wishes to deny any need for gratitude and instead return the compliment to the speaker as in:

Table #5

A:	"Tha-ank you."
B:	"No no-o, thank you-ou."

"English is heavily stressed. For example, *record* and *permit*" (*Teaching Tactics for Japanese English Classrooms* by John Wharton). Although his point is very valid, it is in fact the natural rhythm of the language and would be better explained by pointing out that the natural three-beat rhythm—as in the use of "tha-ank you" or "thank yo-ou"—is often used in other words too, to convey different meanings. The words that Wharton uses are good examples. "Reh-eh-cord" is a noun, but "ree-co-ord" is a verb. "Per-mih-it" is a verb but "peh-er-mit" is a noun.

Rhythm is a section of language acquisition that teachers tend to miss or skip over too quickly, and yet good rhythm aids other areas. In the natural progress of learning, previous levels help subsequent levels; learning them in the correct order makes learning—and, of course, teaching—much easier. Speaking, Reading and Writing rely heavily on Rhythm. Rhythm lessons are therefore essential.

An enjoyable and very effective lesson is had by having the class clap their hands in unison to a regular beat, the speed of which has been preset by the teacher, while the students in turn try to read or say a sentence, scrunching and pulling the words to fit the rhythm. There is no need to tell the student that he is wrong. He knows when he fails to make the correct word fall on the correct beat, and so he knows immediately that he is out.

An example of this would be a sentence written on the board, such as "Mary is learning how to drive so that she can take her dad's car to town." The teacher sets the speed of the clapping. The entire class then says the desired word at each clap, with a fourth clap to signify a break before the next student tries.

Table #6

Clap,	Clap,	Clap,	Clap,
drive	car,	town,	Next!

While the class continues to clap and chant, "drive, car, town, Next!" each student in turn tries to read the sentence so that his "drive" and the "drive" of the class fall together. Much hilarity is had when a student successfully manages to squash Maryislearningtodrive together but then fails to drag out "her Dad's car" to make his "car" and the "car" of the class fall together. With a small class or an adult class, the use of a metronome is a wonderful way to achieve the same result.

Speaking

Make sure that you give your students many examples of speaking. As a native speaker, you have an automatic rhythmic manner of speaking. It is a precious gift. Do not throw it away by speaking slowly or overly clearly and thereby ruining the rhythm. This can happen very easily if you cast yourself into the sole role of teacher. Role playing is an excellent way to ensure that this does not happen. Reading stories to the students is another excellent way to present them with the different ways each character has in expressing himself. Engaging in a little role play from the readings will help students to realize that some expressions are too powerful to be used by some shy, retiring characters and vice versa.

It must always be borne in mind, however, that Speaking is a skill that comes long before Reading. A native English speaker will be very fluent in his own language by the time he learns how to read. Presenting the written word to non-native speakers before they can speak is often a necessary evil, but it is a wrong step, and the teacher must do all that she can to continually present speech to the students rather than text. If the school demands that the students be given texts to read, then storybooks are best. They contain speech, and the speech is chosen to suit the characters in the book. Unfortunately, students are often given textbooks rather than storybooks. They can be used successfully but you must ensure that the English that such books contain is indeed English. Many textbooks contain English that should never have been written, should never be seen, and should certainly not be taught.

Remember: YOU ARE THE EXPERT.

Run every piece of English through your mother/teacher/bar scenarios before you teach it. If you do that, you will be able to reject some of the incredibly bad examples that I have seen in some textbooks.

"This is a pen."

This incredibly bad piece of English has become so common now as to be a joke. But before the native speakers, the experts, woke up to the fact that it was so bad, it was taught to many thousands of unsuspecting students. They rely on you to help them. Remember: YOU ARE THE EXPERT.

Imagine sitting next to someone in a pub in any English-speaking country in the world. Imagine opening your mouth and saying, "This is a glass." The next scene needs little in the way of imagination, but at best, you will receive a reply such as, "Do you think I'm stupid?" Naturally, the less intelligent the person is, the more he will resent being told.

"Is this a pen?"

If you are still mentally in the aforementioned drinking establishment, you will easily imagine the reaction that such a comment is bound to solicit. "Is this a glass?" The replies to this question are varied and colourful! "Is this a beer?" If the barman does not ask you to leave, the bouncer may well do so.

Imagine it used in the classroom.

Student: "Is this a pen?"

Teacher: "Yes. And if you don't hurry up and get on with your work you can use it after school to write out 'I must hurry up' two thousand times."

Whatever scenario you use, this comment will not encourage friendship. Quite the opposite!

"No, it is not a pen."

This is often cited in books as an answer to "Is this a pen?" Running this one through my mind as taking place in a bar or nightclub makes my blood curdle. It does not take a lot of imagination to fill in the retort from someone who asks if this is your seat and you reply with, "No, it is not my seat."

When you feel that English is not quite right, the scenario of a bar will usually let you see very quickly whether any particular phrase or sentence is good. If you are still not sure and still not convinced, imagine your mother's reaction if you said it to her. Or what would your friend say?

Remember: YOU ARE THE EXPERT. You have the ability to run any particular phrase or sentence through many such scenarios. You can conjure up any number of scenarios to test the correctness of the English that you are being asked to teach. This is what makes you the expert. Imagine saying it to your sister, your brother, your boss, or your neighbour. If you are not sure, keep testing it.

"It is a pencil."

This piece of English is normally used in conjunction with the previous question and answer, thereby making up a small dialogue such as:

"Is this a pen?"

"No, it is not a pen. It is a pencil."

Incredible though it may seem, I have actually seen this written down and offered to teachers as a text for teaching English. Using the bar scenario and the chair, it becomes: "Is this your chair?" "No, it is not my chair. It is the club's chair." Providing scenarios for such examples of English is not only educational and insightful—it is often hilarious. Once, during a class, I was explaining to my students (all of them English teachers) why such problems arise and why there is a need to run it through the mother/teacher/bar scenarios. One student, Riho Konishi, who was grateful for the advice said that she had often used it but sometimes needed an even finer test. She pointed out that she was not sure she always tested the English both as spoken by her to a student and by a student to her. I was a little confused. She explained that she found it acceptable, when running the English through the teacher/student scenario, for the student to ask the teacher, "Is this a chair?" When the teacher asks the student, it is very different.

She gave us the following scenario. A teacher enters a classroom to find one of the students sitting on top of a desk. The teacher says, "Is this a chair?"

The student replies, "No, it is not a chair. It is a desk." The scene defies imagination.

"I am going to town."

This is another golden oldie. "Going somewhere?" someone asks.

"I am going to town," replies our poor student of English.

Suddenly, all friendliness is gone as the first person responds with, "Well! Don't let me stop you!"

No one has explained to that poor student that to "open up words" instead of using contractions in such a way is fighting talk. Remember: YOU ARE THE EXPERT. You do not need to know *why* any of these phrases are wrong. You have a lifetime of using and hearing the language. Just find scenarios for the English and KNOW that it is wrong. Leave it to others to work out why it is wrong.

Often the problem is that the student is speaking written English. There are two distinct types of English: written English and spoken English. "We use tautologies often when speaking but the spoken word and the written word are different" (*Improve Your Punctuation and Grammar* by Marion Field). We must remember: SPOKEN ENGLISH CANNOT BE WRITTEN, unless it is put into inverted commas, and WRITTEN ENGLISH CANNOT BE SPOKEN, unless the person is fighting.

A good scenario for this is a young girl talking to her mother.

Table #7

Girl:	I'm going to town.
Mother:	No, you're not.
Girl:	I am going to town
Mother:	No. You are not.

The girl, in an act of defiance, opens up the words "I'm going" to make "I am going." The mother, quite rightly, then opens up her words to emphasise that the child is certainly *not* going to town. Changing these words into written English changes the dialogue and the feelings.

Table #8

Girl:	I'm going to town.
Mother:	No, you're not.
Girl:	I'm going to town.
Mother:	Didn't you hear me? I said you're not.

In this instance, we are not sure if the girl is defying her mother, and the mother is not so sure either. She therefore checks whether the girl innocently failed to register the fact that permission was not going to be granted, but she has not started to be angry yet. She has not opened up her words.

English is an emotional language. This is a most important fact. English speakers, especially Britons, are famous for their straight faces; their stiff upper lips. But this is because there is no need for any sign of emotion on the face. The words, if chosen well, will send over waves of the desired emotion. This can be fairly adequately explained by the following table

Table #9

No feeling	Mild feeling	Strong feeling
:	:	:
:	:	(4) Love
:	(2) Like	:
(1)	:	:
:	(3) Dislike	:
:	:	(5) Hate
:	:	:
:	:	:

When written English is spoken, it falls into the category of strong emotion. This then sends a message of hate to the listener and so a feeling of fighting is conveyed. Japanese people are often surprised and stunned when a native speaker suddenly turns rather nasty, and they are quite at a loss to understand, little knowing that they themselves instigated the attack.

It is not natural for Western people to attack. It is culturally frowned upon and from babyhood the Western person is trained never to hit first but if hit by anyone then to retaliate is natural. I find it easy to explain this point to Japanese students by using the flowers of the countries. The Japanese love the cherry blossom and the chrysanthemum. The cherry blossom offers no resistance. It simply ups and dies at the first puff of wind. Chrysanthemums endure well. Put a bunch of flowers in a vase and the chrysanthemums will remain strong and fresh long after the others have died. Their ability to suffer is also exceptional. I have often neglected to change the water but still these superb flowers stand tall and straight in the vase.

In England, people praise the rose. In Scotland they worship the thistle. Both flowers are attractive to the eye but lethal to the finger. Indeed, the Scottish motto is "No one touches me with impunity"—or, to put it as the Scots do, "Wha daur meddle wi me?" To cite it properly: *nemo me impune lacessit.*

It follows then that if the Western person to whom the non-native speakers are talking becomes angry, it is likely to be in retaliation, and so it is probably the non-native speakers' aggressive English that is causing the friction.

"Yes, I am."

This type of answer is often given in books as the answer to questions such as, "Are you going out?" But again, it is fighting talk. It signifies a strong emotion—that of hate. It is another example of written English being used as spoken English. If it is spoken, it becomes bad English but it is also not very good English even if it is written. It gives off the impression of intense dislike, because it tells the first speaker to stop talking. This is not a very good thing to teach students to do. When I teach teachers how to teach English, I warn them to guard very carefully against this type of conversation. The following examples will explain the point fully.

Example 1 - The One-word Answer

A: Are you going into town?
B: Yes.

This one-word answer tells speaker A to stop talking, because speaker B does not want to engage in conversation. I call it the "Go away" reply. Unfortunately, students pick it up very easily and use it frequently because it is easy to remember and it is the language of the classroom. In the classroom, pupils are not interested in conversation with the teacher; the teacher wants only an answer and is most certainly not interested in entering into conversation with each pupil. To test this explanation of the one-word-answer, think of the following classroom scenario:

Teacher: What is four plus four?

Pupil: Eight.

This is an excellent answer. The teacher does not desire a conversation. She wants the speech exchange to finish right there. This is a definite example of, "Go away. I do not want to talk anymore."

If you are still unconvinced, imagine the same scenario with the pupil expanding the answer.

Teacher: What is four plus four?

Pupil: Eight. And it is interesting that it is always eight regardless of whether it is four elephants plus four elephants or four matchsticks plus four matchsticks.

Example 2 – The Double-answer

This is another offensive, but softer version, of the one-word-answer. The double answer is a single word answer followed by a backup that simply doubles the meaning by echoing the sentiments of the first part of the answer. Answers such as "Yes, I am," or "No, I don't," are double answers. To test the degree of offense given by double answers, consider the following conversation between an EFL student and a neighbour.

Neighbour: Are you going to town?

Student: Yes. I am.

The result is that the neighbour is offended. This single word answer coupled with a confirmation which is simply a reiteration of the first part, is a rejection. Instead of saying, "Go away. I do not want to talk," it sends a message of, "Please go away. I am too tired, or too disinterested to talk." I call this one the "please-go-away" reply.

Both the go-away and the please-go-away replies kill conversation. This is surely not what the student wants. He wants to talk. He wants to stimulate conversation. If conversation is desired, answers must always have riders. To encourage conversation the student must give a one-word-answer, or at least an answer as short as possible, followed by a rider. It is the fact that it is followed by a rider that makes conversation welcome.

Neighbour: Are you going out?

Student: Yes. I'm off to buy a new coat.

The neighbour will then talk about the coat. I call the last part of this reply the rider because it steers speaker A into the course that speaker B wants to pursue—the buying of a coat. An answer that is riderless goes nowhere, because speaker A does not know how to continue.

The following answers to the same question explain clearly how the rider works.

Rider 1 - "today"

Neighbour: Are you going out?

Student: Yes. I'm going to buy a new coat today.

Neighbour: Do you have the day off?

The rider directed the neighbour to talk about the day, not the coat. Having been steered by the word "off" speaker B would continue with an answer such as, "Yes. I worked all over the weekend and so I have the day off today." Conversation is ensured and will continue with both participants talking about Speaker A's work and work schedule. No mention of the coat!

Rider 2 – *"town"*

Neighbour: Are you going out?

Student: Yes. I'm going to buy a new coat today in town.

Neighbour: There is a lovely little boutique opened up recently just down the road.

The rider here directs the neighbour to talk about the area where the student wants to buy her coat. The ability to go to town by bus or train may arise; the proximity of equally well stocked boutiques locally may well arise. There will be no conversation about the coat.

Rider 3 – *"coat"*

Neighbour: Are you going out?

Student: Yes. I'm going into town today to buy a new coat.

Neighbour: I hear that the fashion for coats this year is ankle length. Are you thinking of buying one like that?

This time, the conversation will be about the coat. It will be about the coat because the student steered the conversation that way with the use of the rider "coat." In English the last word is important. Native speakers will actually turn a deaf ear to much of the conversation and just keep in touch by catching the last word.

Often, non-native speakers of English fail to sustain a conversation because they inadvertently cut off the first speaker by using one of the go-away responses. Sometimes, however, they use the wrong rider, thereby inadvertently leading the first speaker off in a different direction.

Occasionally, the student will go on to confuse speaker A even more by returning to the first vein of thought, thereby disregarding her own rider. I have often heard such a thing happen when students are trying to conduct conversations. They start well, but by not heeding their own riders, the conversation very soon grinds to a halt. The following is an example of an own rider being disregarded and then a return to the original thought.

Student: I'm going to buy a coat in town today.

Neighbour: Very nice. The shops will be crowded though due to the school holidays coming to an end.

Student: Yes. I want to buy a thick, warm coat.

This disregard for the rider will not ensure good conversation. When giving students speaking lessons, it is good idea to make speaker A choose the last word before delivering the sentence and to make speaker B say the last word heard before following through with the rest of the conversation.

The three "coat" sentences that were used here as examples for riders are very good for using in listening lessons. It is just as important to teach students to catch the last word when listening to English and to seek clarity if they do not hear it, as it is to teach them to choose their last word carefully when speaking.

"Hello."

This piece of English is almost universally taught, and yet it is so wrong. Running it through our scenarios of mother/teacher/bar, it passes the mother and the bar test but not the teacher one. Even in America where "Hello" or "Hi" is more acceptable than in the UK, it is considered rude to greet a teacher or a boss in this manner. These greetings are only acceptable when talking to an equal or an inferior. "Hello," is what we say when we answer the telephone. It means "Is there any intelligent life form there?" It is shouted into an open door to enquire if anyone is at home. I have even heard it used in a joking manner to inform someone that what the listener has heard them say is utter rubbish. Fortunately, the Japanese use their language in exactly the same way, and so it should be easy to teach and explain to Japanese students. They answer their telephones by saying "*Moshi, moshi,*" and they signify that they have just heard a friend speak utter rubbish by saying to him, "*moshi, moshi.*" And yet, "Hello" is still being taught daily in Japanese schools as a way to greet foreigners!

I have written several small books for very young students of English; the pages are mainly one large picture illustrating the English word or phrase written below it. Book 9, *Good Morning*, starts with a picture of a little boy standing next to a cat and underneath the picture the text reads, "Hello, Stripey." The next page shows the same boy next to a dog with "Hello, Spot" written underneath. The next page shows a teenager delivering newspapers, and underneath is written "Morning, David"; underneath a picture of a teenage delivery boy there is "Morning, Bill." The next three pages show a teenager calling into a three different shops. Underneath the picture of the baker's shop we have, "Good morning, Mr. Evans"; under the picture of the news agent's shop, we have,

"Good morning, Mr. Adams"; and "Good morning, Mr. Cornes" appears under the final grocer's shop. "Hello" is for animals, very young children, or a very, very good friend. The American word *Hi* is much more universally acceptable than the British *Hello*, but nonetheless, many British people, especially older ones, may find it offensive to be greeted in such a manner by a young person.

"What is your name?"

This is another example of bad English that can be found in textbooks and is then taught to students by native speakers. I have often given teachers a dressing down for using this one. It is probably the most used and abused piece of English that I have come across.

When we meet a child it is very natural to say "What is your name?" but it is not used to equals or superiors. Imagine a student saying to a teacher, "What is your name?" In Britain, especially in Scotland, people are more clipped and come to the point more quickly than Americans, but even in Scotland, the most straight forward speaking country of all, it is unacceptable. In 1979 I travelled across America by Greyhound bus from Los Angeles to New York, and the only time I heard "What is your name?" was on the bus. Two young lads had been arguing with each other and were beginning to speak rather loudly. The driver told them to remember that there were other passengers on the bus. I could not hear the lad's reply but the driver followed up with "What's your name?" and was greeted with a string of abuse. Always remember that "What is your name?" directed at an equal or someone older carries an implied threat.

There are only two people who can use that sentence. One is a policeman and the other is a hotel concierge who is looking into the problem of a double-booked room. Even then, the concierge is likely to say, "May I have your name?" Although this is much softer, it still cannot be taught to students.

There is only one way to solicit someone's name and that is to give them your own name first. A good way to remember this is to think of your name as a present. Everyone knows that if you ask for a present, your chances of receiving one are very slim. If you want a present from someone, you have a better chance of receiving it if you give them a present first. Remember, your name is a present. Not everyone may have it.

Example 1 - Student A wants to ask student B for his name.

Table #10

Student A: I'm Joan. Joan MacLean.

Student B: Jim. Jim Cummings (pointing to himself).

or

Student A: "I'm Joan. Joan MacLean."

Student B: "I'm James. Call me Jim."

I teach the first version and only the first version. I do this basically because it is the simplest, the easiest to remember, and the one least likely to cause offence. I teach it by quoting the famous line from the 007 films: "Bond. James Bond." It is easy for me to explain that using the surname twice means that the speaker should be referred to as Mr. Bond, not James. This makes it an excellent example. The James Bond films have done a good job of making sure that my students understand that Mr. Bond, and not James, is the desired response. Had our famous character answered with, "James. James Bond," then he would expect to be called James.

These are but some of the many, many examples of bad English that I have come across in my teaching career. They are so common in Japan that we now call them Japlish. I have no idea who is setting out these examples of absurd English for students to learn, but it is you, the native speaker, the expert, who must stop it. Remember: YOU ARE THE EXPERT. Every piece of English that has been written into a book is suspect. Examine each carefully before you decide to teach it. Students should be conversant in English BEFORE they are ever given any written text—but when teaching in schools, it is almost impossible to achieve this.

"Learning to speak a foreign language (especially when the student's earlier focus has been on writing and reading) takes patience and practice" (*Teaching Tactics for Japanese English Classrooms* by John Wharton). Language learning is personal. We do not all speak the same way. Some people swear and some use coarse imagery. Some people would never use rough words and prefer to paint glowing verbal pictures. Each student must be allowed to use the language to express their own personal preferences. If swearing occurs, I tell the students that they may use it outside but not in front of me, and I suggest that they behave in the same way to any other foreigner who fits my description. After that, there always follows some lively and interesting descriptions of the type of people who would object, who would not like it but would not object, who would not object, and finally, who would use swear words.

It stands to reason that as teachers we must use every opportunity to make the students speak in their own way. But first, we have to help them to speak. If Listening,

Pronunciation, Vocabulary, and Rhythm lessons have all been done, the student is, indeed, ready to speak. Naturally, some very peculiar types of speech emerge. This is normal even in young native English speakers. Every infant teacher has heard children use "teached" and buyed" instead of *taught* and *bought* and another million variations to boot. I once had a little five-year-old in my class, in my own country, who told me once that his mother "splungshed" him. After considerable probing, we discovered that the mother had hit him with a wet sponge. Were these children non-native speakers, we would say that they were speaking pidgin English, when, in fact, they were merely adventuring into unknown spoken territories and conjugating verbs as they thought that they might be or should be—which is, in fact, intelligent supposition.

Once, when I was in South Africa, I went into a bank to cash a cheque. The cashier, a native English speaker, asked me when I would like the cash.

"Now," I answered.

"Well, if you come back at about 2:00 p.m. tomorrow, we will have it ready for you," she said.

I was dumbfounded. Mentally, I ran the conversation through my head again: *"Now." "Come back tomorrow."*

A woman standing beside me in another queue, seeing my perplexity, leaned over and said to the cashier, "The lady wants it now, now."

The cashier looked at me as if I was lacking something and said rather slowly, "If you want the money now, now, I can stamp the cheque for you, and then you need to take it to the teller over there, and he will pay you now, now." Apparently in Johannesburg, "now, now" means right now whereas "now" means "no great hurry, but sometime soon."

All over the world, people speak English, often learned as a second language. And so we have pidgin English. Pidgin English is not a problem if it is seen for what it is. It is simply a stage that all children pass through as they try to make up their own English instead of simply repeating words and phrases that they have heard. Similarly, it is a stage that EFL speakers go through when they try to make up their own English while thinking from a non-English base. We often refer to this stringing words together as "the making of English necklaces."

The children in our nursery are technically studying English as a second language, as they can all speak Japanese before they come to the nursery, but they soon become bilingual. They therefore pass through this pidgin English stage very quickly. In our nursery school, we welcome the phase as a herald of fluent speech. It shows that the children are now trying to make up their own English.

One morning, I had been out to visit another nursery, and when I returned, I popped my head round the door to greet the children who had already arrived. I looked at the two three-year-olds sitting there and said, "Morning."

"Good morning," said Mia.

"Me too," said Tsubaki.

Technically, she was correct. They had been taught that when one child asks for something, the others do not repeat the question, but simply says, "Me too." She was experimenting. One of our other teachers, Lindsay Cameron Kawai, who studied bilingualism and took a Master's in Education specialising in TESOL, identified Tsubaki's problem as overgeneralization.

There are three problems for non-native English speakers: (a) Pidgin English, (b) First Language

Interference and (c) Overgeneralization. . . . Although these are very different problems the answer to all three are the same. All three occurred because the correct pattern was insufficiently practiced. The answer to all three is therefore—masses of practice; i.e., drilling the required phrase or sentence until it automatically becomes used. The difference between the three problems is that in the case of Pidgin English the drilling needs to be twice as much as with the problems of First Language Interference which needs twice as much drilling as is needed in the case of Overgeneralization. (*The Study of Second Language Acquisition* by Rod Ellis)

Although I am unqualified to say how much more practice one area needs than another, I can say that what is being said here is most certainly true. "Drilling the required phrase or sentence until it automatically becomes used" is essential. What we are being told, then, is that the students have to say something again and again and again in order to have the words able to be easily accessed and used. This is very acceptable and very easy to do. Children love drills and will hammer away at a word or a phrase until they have it quite right. An example of a two-year-old:

Patrick then said that his mommy would spank me— "Like this." I pretended to cry. This is an absolutely foolproof game to play with little children; they all love it. Soon we had a game going. The little children would "spank" me—slap me on the back—and I would pretend to cry. When I stopped Patrick would say, "I'm still spanking you" and I would have to start again. Now and again I would say, "I'm a good boy."

He would say, very firmly, "You bad boy." And so we went on for some time. . . .

Lisa remembers and likes to use phrases that carry some emotional weight. Within the past few weeks, I have heard her say for the first time, "No fair!" "I'm making a mess!" "Don't make me mad!" and "Quit it!" (*How Children Learn* by John Holt)

When another child, a baby, was playing the piano, Holt, in order to prevent any damage to the instrument, closed the controls door, saying, "Let's get this out of the way."

This too became part of his regular routine. Every so often, when playing, he would close this cover and say, "Let's get this out of the way." . . .

Another child was banging out a whole string of letters at top speed on a typewriter when all at once he said, "Oops! I made a mistake." (*How Children Learn* by John Holt)

These children are simply practicing and trying to use what they have heard. Adults will often do the same. One English language teacher, who married her student, often told the story of how her husband nearly brought the marriage to a halt by his excessive usage of the word *horrible*. He applied it daily to almost all situations as he tried and tested his newfound treasure.

To drill and drill and drill is the answer. But how? This is where the good teacher will use classroom games. For instance, there is a game called I Went Out to Dinner. With this game the first student says, "I went out to dinner and I had roast beef."

The second student follows on by saying, "I went out to dinner and I had roast beef and salad."

The third student says, "I went out to dinner and I had roast beef, salad, and green peas," and so on.

Any student who does not remember what was said, or who remembers the menu wrongly is out. The game is pleasurable, an essential part of the plan, and it covers three areas at the same time. It quite obviously covers vocabulary, but it also drills to perfection the fact that in English grammar, a list of articles separates each item with a comma, and there is only one "and" which comes in just before the last item. It also—and this is the aim of the game—lets the students say and hear others saying a million times, "I went out to dinner and I had . . . "

The game can be changed to cover almost any vocabulary situation. "I went swimming and I took a . . . " can be used with all items deemed necessary for a swimming trip until even fantastic items are used. One student I had was stuck for another item and finished by saying, "and a magic wand." This, of course, added to the hilarity of the game and was naturally well remembered. Medical variations are possible too, as in, "I went skiing and broke my arm/sprained my ankle/etc." Because the variations to this game are endless, the students are willing to play it almost every lesson. Perfect for the few minutes left to fill at the end of a period!

One final word on speaking is that we must be aware that what we say in English need not be correct, because we often say what we do not mean. As native speakers, we have grown up with adults saying one thing but meaning another. I can clearly remember my mother, with love shining out of her eyes, saying to me whenever I asked too many questions, or ones that were too difficult, "Oh, Maud! Go and play under the buses!" It made me laugh, but I knew that it was time to go elsewhere and annoy someone else. Another of her favourite sayings, whenever I made a mess or broke something, was, "Oh, Maud! I'd give you away, but nobody would take you." Never did I doubt my mother's love. I knew exactly what she meant.

Table #11

"Are you deaf?"	meant	"Do as I tell you."
"Do you think I'm daft?"	meant	"I don't believe it."
"On your bike."	meant	"No."
"Put your money where your mouth is."	meant	"Do it. Don't just talk about it."
"You're daft as a brush and twice as hairy."	meant	"You're being silly."
"You could talk the hind legs off a donkey."	meant	"Be quiet!"

Children master this type of nonsense English very quickly. It may even be they who invented it.

> Her (a child making a jigsaw) way of playing with the puzzle was to take a piece, any piece at all, stick it into what was obviously an impossible place, look around, and make a kind of isn't-that-silly? giggle. . . . To look at something and deliberately call it something else was a good joke. (*How Children Learn* by John Holt)

When this happens, the child is learning to speak our nonsense-type English whereby one adult looks at another adult and thinks *Utter nutter!* but says, "Silly girl." The child hearing this looks at the recipient, a rather mature lady, and thinks *Girl? Silly?* Children use language in this manner too, but rather than modifying it to suit the other person, they use it to suit themselves

An example from our nursery: Yuri Sato (two years old) had just joined our nursery three days previously. She was a little dynamo on legs, and she wanted to be the boss dynamo. Riki Okamoto (three years old) had already been at the nursery for almost a year, and he was having none of this. On each of the three days that Yuri was at the nursery, she tried to tell Riki just what she thought of him. As she could not speak English, she would let rip in Japanese. No sooner had she uttered her first word at him than he and all the other children would stop what they were doing and say to her triumphantly, "Don't speak Japanese!" Yuri was furious.

On the fourth day, Yuri was just about to pull something out of Riki's hand when she caught my eye watching her. She knew the rule about not snatching things from one another. She immediately turned to Riki and shouted, "Don't speak Japanese!" All the other children joined in. Riki began to cry and Yuri swaggered off. In the afternoon, Riki was again warned by the rest of the class not to speak Japanese, and again he cried. Again Yuri swaggered off. This needed investigating.

I hovered near Yuri for almost an hour to find out what Riki was saying to earn this rebuke. Suddenly, Yuri turned to Riki and shouted, "Don't speak Japanese!"

Riki was about to cry and the rest of the children were about to join in the chorus when I held up my hand and said, "Yuri, Riki didn't speak Japanese." Riki smiled a grateful, watery smile. Yuri simply shrugged her shoulders and swaggered off. Her "Don't speak Japanese" meant "Don't annoy me," "Take that!" and/or "I hate you."

All children use their limited language to say just what they want to say, regardless of what it actually means. A good example of this was Yuri's sister, Sakura, who had joined the nursery at the same time. Being a year older, she quickly mastered "Don't speak Japanese" and other relevant phrases. "No falling down!" was one piece of English that fascinated her. I think that she understood it but could not believe it. However, she soon realised what it meant. When children fall, they often cry because the fall frightened them, because they did not understand what happened, because they wonder if someone did something to them, or because falling down prevented them from catching the person they were chasing. They seldom cry because they are hurt.

In the nursery, we deal with this by saying automatically, when a child falls, "No falling down!" This makes them laugh, and they immediately stand up and resume whatever they were doing. If they fall down outside and blood appears, they are very frightened, and so they sometimes do not stop immediately on hearing "No falling down." When this is the case, I tell them to come to me. This warns staff to stay away from the child. They know very well the dangers of picking up a fallen child. They know the damage that can be done by adults picking up a child with an injury. A child who can stand up and come over to me is uninjured. When the child comes over to me, I pretend to suck out the pain. With cheeks full of air, I look questioningly at another child. The fallen child then gleefully points to someone else and I blow out the pain to give it to that child, or teacher, or mother, whoever was indicated. This brings laughter to all and tears are forgotten.

Sakura loved this ritual, especially the "No falling down!" part. As soon as a child fell down, she would rush over and with finger wagging in admonishment she would say angrily, "No falling down!"

One day I was standing in front of Yuri and Mia and asking angrily, while looking at a pool of water on the floor, "Who made this mess?" Sakura, being the big sister, naturally wanted to come to Yuri's defence. She came running over, but when I asked her what she wanted, she looked from Mia to Yuri and, with a puzzled shake of her head, looked up at me. Her English was not up to the standard she needed. She said, "Yuri falling down? Mia falling down?" She meant, "Are you angry at Mia or are you angry at Yuri?" This, after less than a week at the nursery, was exceptionally good use of English, and so it was readily accepted.

I replied. "I don't know yet, but one of them has just spilled the water on the floor, and I am not happy." She nodded her head wisely, turned and left.

In the beginning, all English is acceptable. I have never heard a new mother say to her new baby, who is babbling away, "Oh, I don't understand you. Speak clearly," or "You obviously need to study harder. You are making no sense." Indeed, I have often heard a mother, after hearing her baby say, "Bah wah wah wah," turn and tell the admiring audience that the baby wants to be fed, or wants a biscuit, or some other obviously ridiculous translation of the noises. But every mother then turns to her baby with glowing eyes, praising him for his efforts and saying, "So my little boy wants a biscuit, does he?" or words to that effect.

The baby, encouraged by her loving response says, "Bah wah wah wah," again. This time, he probably means, "You're a stupid-looking ignoramus. I want you to lift me up." Neither the mother nor I know what he is trying to say. We both know, however, that he is trying to speak—and that is praiseworthy. Teachers must remember that all efforts are praiseworthy.

If a teacher asks a question such as, "What colour is an elephant?" and the student answers "Pink," the teacher must not negate the answer. The teacher is supposed to be teaching English, not biology. If the teacher asks a question in English and the student replies in English, the teacher should be grateful! The teacher asked a question in English asking for a colour. The student replied in English giving, quite correctly, the name of a colour. The teacher should be doubly grateful! Besides, I have seen many pink elephants in toy shops. Some teachers may even have seen numerous pink elephants running around a room at the end of a very good party. The teacher should always try to accept every answer if it is delivered in English. In the situation above, it would be good for the teacher to say, "Yes," and then add, "I have seen many pink elephants in toy shops, but I meant elephants in zoos."

Reading

As a primary school teacher, I have spent many, many hours listening to children reading. More often than not, it truly fits the description I once read of "children barking at the print." This is true of native English-speaking children, but much more true of students of English as a second language, even though they are adults. For this reason, lessons on reading are essential.

Here the native-English-speaking teacher shines. You are the expert. You have listened to stories being read to you by your mother or father, your teacher, and even by friends who wished to read out to you some item of news in the local paper. Barking at the print cannot be allowed, and yet, I often hear it being accepted in schools. It must be stopped. It is so easy to stop that it is always a shock to hear it still being done.

The first thing that students have to learn, when learning to read, is that they must do their "finger reading" first. "Finger reading" is when the student runs his finger over the words in the next sentence, mentally reading them, to give himself a chance to know what is coming. He then returns to the beginning of the sentence and reads aloud. This simple lesson is soon mastered and it is very effective in putting an end to students "barking at the print."

Another grave fault is the flatness with which many students read. Not all students have the gift of breathing excitement into the print, but they should be taught to read what the author wrote. The ability to read words in capital letters is essential, such as titles or even words in the middle of a piece of text such as, "Phyllis started to walk but she realized that she was going to have to RUN if she wanted to reach the bus stop in time." Many students do not know—they may never have been taught—how to read words in capital letters. This is an unfortunate state of affairs, because only one lesson on the reading of capital letters is normally all that is required. As soon as the students realize that the natural three-beat rhythm of the sentence is broken up into three threes by the use of capital letters they have no more problems.

Without capital letters the rhythm of the sentence can be shown as

Table #12

Phyllis started to walk
but she realized that she was going to have to run
if she wanted to reach the bus stop in time.

When *run* is written in capital letters, the rhythm changes and becomes:

Phyllis

started to walk

but she realized that she was going to have to

RU

U

Un

if she wanted

to reach the bus stop

in time.

Of course, each beat within the three-beat phrases must be exactly the same length, and so in the sentence above, some phrases would need to be pulled and some would need to be squashed to fit it correctly.

Phy...................ll...........................is

Sta.................rted..................... t'walk

but she realized that she was going t'have t'

R...U

.....U

...Un

if she......... wan............ted

t'reach....... the bus ....stop

in ti...........i.................me.

Similarly, titles of stories or texts take on, in exactly the same way, an extended three-beat rhythm. This then pulls out and exaggerates the small words in titles which would be almost unheard in normal text.

<u>Example</u>:

Table #13

"The school pond in winter," written in normal text, would be:

The school

pond

in winter.

When used as a title and written in capital letters, it is read as:

T~H~E

SCH~OO~L

(pause)

(pause)

(pause)

P~O~ND

(pause)

(pause)

(pause)

I- ~ -N

WI~NT~ER.

The pauses and the extended parts of the words need not be long. In fact, they can be very short, but they must be there, and they must be clear.

When reading sentences ending with a question mark, the voice should lift. This lifting of the voice need not be at the end of the sentence, but that is as good a place as any. The lifting of the voice informs the listener of the question. Good readers will often lift the voice at some other appropriate place in the sentence to show the part of the sentence that is indicating the question.

Native speakers will often use a solitary word and make it have different meanings by the rise or fall of the voice. A wife who says "Tea?" to her husband, with a slow lifting of her voice expects an answer because she is asking him if he would like some tea. The slow delivery coupled with the rising tone of her voice informs him of this. The wife who says "Tea!" to her husband with a quick falling of her tone expects him to put down his paper or whatever he is doing and come to the table immediately. Although the speech was unseen, only heard, the husband knew that there was a question mark after the first delivery and an exclamation mark after the second one.

Exclamation marks need to be heard by the listener. The student who is reading a passage and comes across an exclamation mark need not read it quickly and with a falling tone, but the listener must be informed of the exclamation mark, and this is done by changing the power of the voice. Any text preceding an exclamation mark is read in a louder voice than the rest of the text. Although not essential, it also helps if the reader can speed up the delivery.

Text written in italics is indicated by raising the pitch of the voice when reading. There is no need to read in a soprano voice, but the rise in pitch will allow the listener to hear the italics.

When the reader comes to the end of a sentence that ends in a period, there should be a three-beat pause. This allows the listener to draw the sentence to a close, secure the meaning of the last word heard, and prepare to take in the meaning of the words coming next. A comma in text is read aloud with three beats before the comma and three beats after it. The reader must make sure that the rhythm is changed to mirror the insertion of the comma.

New Progress in English Book 2 by Robert M. Flynn has a passage which I have used countless times when helping students who have difficulty in reading. Even the title is useful. It is called "Thank You, Japan."

Table #14

Without the comma, it reads:

Thank

You

Japan.

With the comma it reads:

Tha...

ank

you,

Ja

pa

an.

The students read it at first as if it was written without a comma. Having explained the rhythm change required by the comma, they then read it again as it would be read if it were not a title. Finally applying what they learned regarding the need of words written in capital letters, to have three beats per word it becomes:

Table #15

Tha....a.....a.

a.........a....nk

y...o....u......,

Pause

Pause

Pause

J......a........a

pa.....a.......a

a...............n.

The rest of the passage is equally good and by the time we have reached the end of the page the students are well aware of how English should be read. There is, of course, a great deal of hilarity to the lesson and because it is such fun, the lesson is not forgotten. Thereafter, there is no more barking at the print.

This reading of three beats between commas with three-beat pauses after a period is carried on through into our notation system. In large numbers, there are three figures between commas and when we reach the point (or period), we change our rhythm slightly and read each number with a three-beat pause after it.

Normally, teachers, when teaching reading to EFL students, will have students who are able to read in their own language, and so the obstacles will be only those that have been outlined above. If, however, you are expected to teach reading to children who have not yet started to read any language then there are some rules that need to be followed.

"We readers have the expert's eye for significant detail; the child does not" (*How Children Learn* by John Holt). This is one of the first problems for young children. For them, there is little or no difference between an "n" and an "h." Doing jigsaws gives children this insight to significant detail. To this end, I have amassed a huge pile of jigsaws which I have numbered in order of difficulty. Only when the child is able to do the last one do I decide to start him on reading. The first reading books should be storybooks featuring pictures and simple text. The child will simply memorize the text and apply it to the picture. This is excellent, and this is reading. To start children reading by teaching them the alphabet is meaningless. Naming the letters and knowing in which order they occur in the alphabet belongs in the realm of Spelling. Teaching a child to spell before he can read or write is not only extremely silly, it causes a great deal of confusion that teachers need to iron out later.

Children need to start their reading adventure with books, with stories, with English that carries a meaning. "One of the reasons why children from unlettered homes are at such a disadvantage when they start learning to read may be that they lack this familiarity with the shapes of words and letters" (*How Children Learn* by John Holt). This is indeed the truth but we must also be aware that children from unlettered homes have not had their interest in Reading sparked. I have taught young children to read for almost forty years, and I have found that some children from lettered and some children from unlettered homes made jigsaws easily, but the children from unlettered homes had no interest in reading. They did not seem to know what reading was or why we did it. For them, not only was the making of jigsaws essential, but they also had to have stories read to them to show them the pleasures that written words hold.

"It will probably help many children get started in reading if their parents read aloud to them. However, this isn't some kind of magic pill, and if the reading isn't fun for both parent and child, it will do more harm than good" (*How Children Learn* by John Holt). Holt is both right and wrong in what he says. It *is* a magic pill. But if the reading is not fun, then the power of the magic will be greatly diminished. Children who have never had stories read to them are at an enormous disadvantage. Reading to children and making it fun is the most powerful magic available. This magic works well for adults, too.

The difference in reading aloud to children and reading aloud to adults is in the length of the passage that can be read. When reading aloud to young children, the teacher is able to read a whole story—even a whole book—at one sitting. When reading to adults, the passage must be kept short and interesting. Reading out articles from a newspaper and then having a small discussion on each one is an excellent way to ensure that adult classes are exposed to Reading aloud, which is essential, while holding their interest and not giving them the feeling of being insulted.

All first infant classes need to have a library where the children can simply look at the text in books with no pressure on them to have to read. "For children who had hardly ever seen any, this casual looking at books was a sensible and almost certainly a necessary first step to reading" (*How Children Learn* by John Holt). Children learn so much by doing this.

I once had a child who informed me that she could read her big brother's book. As the big brother was ten years old, I had my doubts. The child opened the book and read "Good," from the first page, skipped the next page, and read "Good," from the page after that.

I asked her why she had not read anything from the previous page.

She looked at me as though I were mentally challenged and, in a tone that implied it, said, "There was no 'good' on that page." She was correct. The word *good* did not appear on the second page.

This ability to read the word *good* on different pages and in different positions on the page is a skill in its own right. This is the process by which children follow the text when you read them a story. It never fails to amaze me that children who cannot yet read can tell immediately when you omit or misread a word in a story. They can also point their finger at exactly where the word should have been. They seem to have a mental jigsaw-type image of the printed page.

"Nora misread a word that previously she had read correctly" (*How Children Learn* by John Holt). The road to good reading is never smooth. Children have many setbacks. Sometimes, they seem to forget a word that they previously knew. This is natural, and it happens with both infant readers and adult readers alike when trying to read unfamiliar words.

When teaching teachers how to teach Reading, I spend a considerable amount time on this phenomenon. I explain to them that if they were to meet their doctor on the ski slope they would have great difficulty in recognizing him. When the children or even adult non-native readers meet the same word on a different page on a different line, buried in a different string of words, then it is different. It is not the same. We do not read each individual letter in a word. We do not even read each individual word.

I have lost the original text that I used for my teachers when teaching this particular lesson, but I have reconstructed it from memory to the best of my ability.

Table #16

"The polar bear differs from the great panda in many different ways. One of the the greatest differences is, of course, in the colour of the animals. Whereas the one is totally white, the other is very clearly black and white and has a well-known pattern. Their are many other differences, too, but these are masked by the fact that the colours of the animals are so different that they claim all of your attention. In both bears there ears are totally different shapes."

I then ask the teachers to find the mistakes in the passage. Most teachers find only two mistakes. This is because they are reading the passage as a whole. Proofreading is the skill that is being called upon here and proofreading is a totally different skill from reading. It follows then that there are several types of reading: Proofreading, Reading silently for pleasure or information, and Reading out loud. Many teachers mistake the essential quality of Reading out loud.

> *Gyns at Wrk* by Glenda Bissex . . . at the start of the preface she writes: This is an account of one child learning to read and write . . . . When I began taking notes about my infant son's development I did not know that I was gathering "data" for "research" . . . . When I speculated aloud that his early oral reading had been aimed at receiving adult feedback and correction, he argued instead that *he* needed to hear the sounds in order to know if they were right. (*How Children Learn* by John Holt)

Children never fail to amaze nor teach us. Everyone who has ever spoken a foreign language knows how it feels to utter the foreign words with the differently shaped mouths and tongues and how it feels to hear oneself say these words. All students of a foreign language need lots of practice in speaking out loud and in reading out loud.

Reading Rules

The silent "e" rule

There are many rules in Reading, and one of the most often quoted one is the silent "e." I always advise against the use of the phraseology "silent e." I think that it misleads the students. Students, adults and children alike, seem to understand it better when told that it is a "magic e" and that the "magic e" changes the vowel and makes it say its own name. Having done its work, it is then free and can go off to bed. This sentence appeals to young and old alike, and because they like it, they remember it. This is an important point. For learning to take place at maximum efficiency teachers and children must both have fun.

The double-letter rule

Teaching the "magic e" rule paves the way for this second part of the rule, i.e. the double-letter rule. To explain this rule to the students, I ask them to add "-ing" to a list of words. In doing so, they must make use of the double-letter rule: a word must have two letters between vowels. Simply hearing this rule once opens a massive door for them, and they almost all handle *bid* to *bidding*, *sit* to *sitting* and *hand* to *handing* with little or no problem. As soon as this rule is shown to them, students immediately start running mental lists of words through their heads. This is, of course, an excellent start to the lesson. When students find out something for themselves, they remember it well!

This sets the groundwork so well for them that when they are shown *bide* and *site,* almost no teaching is required. They immediately see for themselves that "bideing" and "siteing" are unacceptable and so the "magic e" is dropped—but prior to dropping it, there are two letters between the two "i's." This part of the rule, however, really belongs under the heading of grammar and will be dealt with more fully in that section.

Table #17

Rule A: There should always be two letters between two sounding vowels. If there is only one letter, then it must be doubled prior to adding "-ing."

Rule B: Adding an "e" to the end of a word makes the vowel say its own name.

Rule C: When adding "-ing" to a word with an "e" at the end, the "e" is dropped.

Rule D: If a word has a double letter, then the vowel will say its natural sound. If the word has a single letter then the word will have a vowel that says its own name.

A	B	C	D
hat	hatting	hate	hating
bed	bedding	bede	beding
sit	sitting	site	siting
rob	robbing	robe	robing
cub	cubbing	cube	cubing
hand	handing		

A	B	C	D
bend	bending		
silt	silting		
bond	bonding		
punt	punting		

They can then fold the paper to show the lists headed by "hatting" and "hating" lying together, learned because the teacher was following the advice of Confucius: "I hear and I forget; I see and I remember; I do and I understand."

To help young children read quickly and efficiently, I have written some books that take them gently and surely through the early stages while making sure that the English therein is good English and suitable to be used by them. Although we insist that the children in our nursery school are five years old before we begin formal reading, many teach themselves prior to our commencement. We do not encourage it because children do not have binocular vision much before seven years old, and so we hold off reading until they are five—but if they show interest, we do not dissuade them. We help them, but only if they ask.

One child in our nursery started reading long before she was ever given books. Yuri Sato, two years old, was fascinated by the signs hanging on the outside of the toilet doors. They can be turned to show "engaged" or "vacant." These are used because the children are not allowed to lock the toilet doors. Most children learn to read these signs and some others that we have around the nursery. Yuri quickly learned to read quite a few words, but they were always of her own choosing. Her name was one of her chosen words.

In the nursery, each child has a mat to use in order to protect the floor when they draw with crayons. Their name is clearly written on the mat and each child very quickly is able to identify his or her own name and thereby lay claim to the correct mat. One day, Yuri had no mat, because earlier in the day she had made a plasticine dog and I had left it on her mat for her mother to see at the end of the day. When Yuri complained about having no mat, I gave her mine.

When the lesson was finished the children cleared up and went to prepare themselves for lunch. One mat was left lying on the floor. "Who left this mat lying here?" demanded the teacher in charge.

Everyone looked at Yuri, and some children started to say, "Yuri, Yuri," to tell her to go and pick up the mat, but Yuri was having none of it.

The teacher said, "Yuri, that's your mat. Go and pick it up."

Feeling righteously indignant, Yuri marched over to the mat and looked at it for a few seconds, decided that she was looking at it upside down and marched round to the other side. She gazed at it for a while and then triumphantly put her hands on her hips and walked away, saying loudly, "Mrs. Ramsay's mat!" Yuri had learned to read!

Writing

Neither children nor adults can write until they have mastered the formation of the letters. This makes Penmanship a necessary part of writing lessons. Spelling, on the other hand, has nothing to with the Writing category. Spelling, along with Dictation, comes later under the heading of Grammar.

"A child will write down anything and be content that it says what he wanted it to say" (*How Children Learn* by John

Holt). This is a common occurrence. When my niece started school at five years old, her younger sister, then only four years old, was anxious to start school, too, but the powers-that-be refused her entry. The older niece gloated in her newfound glory.

One day the older child sat down, laboriously wrote out a sentence, and then took it to her father. Her father read out the note and congratulated her, telling her how clever she was. The older niece smirked. The younger niece glowered. Not to be outdone, the younger child took a piece of paper and a pencil and wrote on it. Now she, in her turn, flounced over to her father and handed him the piece of paper, whereupon she turned to her sister and smirked as she waited for her father to read the message aloud.

Her father gazed at the scribbles on the piece of paper, and then, with sudden insight, he handed it back to her and said, "Good girl. Read it out to us, please."

She turned angrily to him and said, "You know I can't read!"

So often, children cannot read back what they have written. Neither can the teacher. The children in our nursery write constantly. Sometimes I can read what they think they have written or what they intended their letters to convey. Sometimes I cannot. When I ask them what they wrote, they sometimes shrug and simply say, "I don't remember."

"Children like Julia could write prolifically at the responsibility-free scribble stage. But the next step proved to be a traumatic one for some of the writers, as they realized that their readers could not in fact read their scribbles" (*How Children Learn* by John Holt). As long as the child is not made to feel that he has in some way failed to achieve something then there is no problem at all in the fact that others cannot read their scribbles.

When I ask our nursery school children what they have written, they happily tell me what they wrote and I write it in properly for them. When they cannot remember what they wrote, I suggest things or make up what it could have been. Sometimes the children accept my suggestions. Sometimes they do not. The scribbles of most of our nursery school children consist of bundles of characters that sometimes approximate words, as in "5 earzs od." But sometimes they do not. Again, this is no problem. At best, they have been writing a story. At worst, they have been turning the laborious task of penmanship into a skill that they have used in order to try to achieve another aim.

"It can't be said too often: we get better at using words, whether hearing, speaking, reading, or writing, under one condition and only one—when we use those words to say something we want to say to people for purposes that are our own" (*How Children Learn* by John Holt). To do this with the written word, children first have to master penmanship.

This is such an enormous task that I have written twenty books in a series to help teachers who are teaching penmanship. The books range from the start of nursery to the end of university. Each book is geared to the level of the child at each stage. It is often assumed that by the time a student reaches the end of university, he is able to write all of the letters of the alphabet, and so Penmanship is a needless task. Far from it. If encouraged, the students' natural interest grows, and calligraphy awaits.

At nursery level, the books that I have written are probably no better than many such books that can be found on the market. All that I can really say in defence of them is that they fit perfectly into the rest of the penmanship scheme that I have created. They concentrate on the hand movements that are necessary for children at that stage, and they use different writing implements according to the age of the child. The very young child should not be asked to hold a pencil. Not only is it dangerous, but his little hands are too fat and podgy to grip it properly, resulting in frustration rather than pride. The very young need fat implements such as crayons.

In primary school stages, the books guide the students through the letters required in a manner that breeds success. It cannot be said often enough that success smells sweet and failure stinks. A teacher's job is to present material chopped up small enough for students to be able to bite, but sliced thickly enough for them to be able to have a good chew. In that way, the students move from success to success.

The letters of the alphabet in this series are presented in an order to facilitate ease of formation.

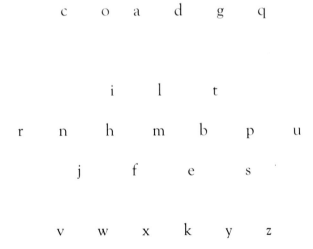

And they are all lowercase letters. Students just beginning penmanship have no need of capital letters. So often, I see poor little students just starting school trying to master two alphabets: uppercase and lowercase. This only leads to confusion.

Twenty-six letters are more than enough for one year of study. Besides, in normal everyday English we hardly ever use capital letters. The first grader certainly has no use for them at all, other than for that of his first name.

The book for second-year primary school students makes use of upper and lowercase letters, and the students write the texts using fountain pens. This adds a new skill to their budding adroitness. Attached is an example of the penmanship of a nine-year-old child using a fountain pen. Although Kana's work was the best, most of the children wrote beautifully.

> 18·6·2011 Penmanship 7
>
> i p i p i p i p i p
>
> Painting pictures is
>
> fine. Practicing
>
> Penmanship is better.
>
> Practicing both is fine

Each level introduces something new. When the university levels are reached, the student who has made his way through all levels will have covered linked script and will have used different slants and different writing implements. At university level, the students are encouraged to investigate their own preferred styles and slants and go on to signatures. It is amusing to see university students still writing diligently, still practicing their own signatures, long after I have told them that the lesson is finished. No need to set homework for these students. They greedily seek it for themselves.

Having achieved the ability to write the letters of the alphabet without having to stop and think about each letter, it is time for the pupils to use their newfound skills to write stories, essays, and compositions.

Composition

To this end, I made up a book full of pictures. Each child uses the book differently according to his age and ability. The transitions from spelling isolated words to writing them into a composition is very difficult and can produce much hilarity for the teacher as she tries to wrestle with what has been written.

One child wrote a very passable composition, but near the end he wrote, "The boy asked his Mummy for some money. 'MEC,' said the mother."

I was puzzled. I asked if the mother was trying to spell a word or signify some kind of code.

The boy was puzzled by the question. Eventually, he told me that the mother did not know what to answer, so she was thinking, but he did not know what she was thinking.

Neither did I. "Okay," I answered, "you read me the story." I hoped to pick up something from his inflexion. I certainly did.

He read: "The boy asked his Mummy for some money. 'Let me see,' she said."

For very young children, I provide a picture and tell them to draw the picture. I then talk to them about the picture to show them that they conveyed information to me by this method. After I made a book full of pictures for children to use, I made another book about how to teach composition. The teacher learns the process from helping a child convey a story by the use of a picture, up to the level of helping the adults to do the same thing.

Japanese students of English tend to write English compositions in exactly the same way as they would write a Japanese composition. I often have to tell them that what I want is an English composition. They nod as though what I am saying hardly needs mentioning. When I continue, "I do not want a translation of what is in your Japanese head," they are instantly alert. *What is this? What is the teacher saying? Is there any other way?*

One of the problems of translating a Japanese story into English is that in Japanese the beginning of the word, the beginning of the sentence, the beginning of the story, is what is important. One of my friends lectures in the art of writing and conducts a class in Writing at one of the local universities here in Osaka. She says that the students are all quite hung up on the fact that they must start with a great sentence—that they must, in fact, make that first sentence into a hook in order to ensnare the reader. In English it is the end of the word, the end of the sentence, the end of the story that is important.

To jolt them out of their Japanese format, I explain that to write a good English story they should do it to this formula: 2D, 3D, 4D. This is easily remembered, and easily understood once I explain that 2D is simply a flat piece of paper. For this part, you must simply draw a picture—a verbal picture. This is where their earlier training has been leading. This, I tell them, is the introduction. For the centre part of the story, bring the picture up into three dimensions. Make the characters come to life. Make them act out the story. Finally, for 4D, I explain, "The terminology 'four dimensions' does not exist. Neither does the end of your story. It is simply an original idea that is in your head and only in your head. It is unable to be conceived by any other person. Surprise me at the end of your story."

One of my students, Benedicte Maemoto, who teaches at a junior secondary school, found an excellent example of what the students are expected to do. The passage was about an all-girls pop group, AKB48, and so it was topical and interesting—and the 4D was a whopper.

Table #18

Who is the Cute Girl in the Centre of AKB48?

The all girl idol group, AKB48, whose members number over 50, is a hot topic these days. Their CD singles were the first and second best selling in Japan over the past six months. In June an election was held in which fans voted for their favourite members of the group. Those members who were ranked within the top 12 now have more opportunities to appear in the media. MAEDA Atsuko was ranked first. Since the right to vote was only given to those who purchased an AKB48CD, some fans purchased quite a few in order to vote for their favourite idol. After the vote, a commercial for Ezaki Glico Co., Ltd. (a leading food manufacturer), was broadcast that caused quite a bit of fuss: in the commercial a super cute unknown girl called EGUCHI Aimi appeared in the centre of AKB48. Later it was disclosed that the girl was created with CGI using the best features of six idols. (*Hiragana Times*, issue 298, August 2011 edition)

One lesson citing 2D, 3D, and 4D, using an example such as the one above, normally ensures good—or at least well-laid-out—compositions from everyone.

Grammar

Spelling is probably the simplest part of grammar and therefore the best place to begin. Most Japanese students leave high school with an extremely high command of English grammar—often far in excess of that of the native speaker, who, because of his ability to simply speak his own native tongue, can find himself cast unwittingly into the role of teacher to some very sophisticated students. It can often be very embarrassing. With spelling, it is fairly straightforward, and therefore fairly safe.

Spelling

The problem is how to teach spelling. Here, the baby is not much help. None of us learned to spell while we were babies. The best teacher for us in this instance then must be the very youngest children at school who are learning how to spell.

In our little nursery school I have set up a system for spelling that the children enjoy. I have recorded my own voice, to which they have become accustomed, dictating the words for spelling, ten at a time, and I have saved them onto the computer. The children enjoy the sophistication of writing out their spelling from the computer. For this reason alone, it is successful. It is not easy to inject a dollop of fun into spelling lessons, but this method does so.

For the older children, to whom computer access holds no charm, I dictate the spelling and then tell them to pass their papers on one space; the child sitting next to them corrects the work. They enjoy this. They feel empowered by the use of the red pen.

For adult classes, I have words written separately on small pieces of paper. I then read out one word and everyone writes it down. When everyone has done this, I spell the word, and the students correct their own work. I then ask one student to read out the next word, which everyone writes, and then I ask the student to spell it. The adults enjoy the fact that no one knows how badly they did. They do, however, always find a way of letting the teacher know whenever they have done well.

"I would simply say, 'Look again' and give them another glimpse . . . . (All these words came from their own papers, the only way to work on spelling that makes any sense at all)" (*How Children Learn* by John Holt). Holt may think that using only words from the students' own papers is the only way that makes sense and indeed it does make sense. I have made great use of that method, but as teachers employed by schools, we are often given a list by the school that employs us, and we must make sure that the children can spell all of the words on the list. Making use of both methods makes better sense.

When I have a list of words that the students must learn, I make a copy of the list for each student, and I highlight the words that the student has spelled correctly. This way, I can see at a glance who needs more help with spelling and where exactly that help is needed. When a student lags behind in spelling, it is then an easy matter to give him the list and tell him to make sure that he can spell at least another three words on that list. This method has never failed me, and no student, in all my years of teaching, has failed to pass more than the three set words at the next test.

Danger! Never be tempted to give the student more than three words to learn. Herein lies the secret. Every student KNOWS that he can learn three words from the list; which words he learns and whether he learns more than three are his choice, and choice is the magic ingredient. It works every time. Students also like to see their list being brightly coloured as the year progresses, and they tend to take a pride in actively playing a part in ensuring that the coloured portions mount satisfactorily.

Vocal spelling is another, but quite different, aspect of spelling and it too should be covered. It should not be assumed that vocal spelling is simply replacing the pen and paper with a voice. It is not. There is more to it than that. When spelling vocally, care must be taken to ensure that the spelling is rhythmic. The word *horse* should be grouped HOR-S-E. Spelling *horse* as H-O-R-S-E is unacceptable.

Rhythm is not the only previous learning area called into play with vocal spelling. Every area is used and therefore needs to be revised. Listening is the first skill in Language acquisition. The students must listen to the words and must listen to the spelling of these words. It is amazing how many students cannot write down a word that is spelled to them vocally. They are also very surprised to find out how much easier it is to write down the word when it is spelled rhythmically.

As they say the letters, their Pronunciation becomes important. It must be clear whether they are saying "b" or "v" and even sometimes "a" or "e." This is an excellent time to introduce the International Radiotelephony Spelling Alphabet used by pilots. Give the students the list for each word used for each letter of the alphabet and explain that the method of using the pilot's alphabet differs from the usual method of clarifying which letter was used. For example, in the pilot's alphabet, *cat* is Charlie Alpha Tango, but everyday situations might be rendered as 'c' for currant, 'a' for apple, and 't' for tiger. It is also wise to inform the students that they should never use country names or town names when using the latter method, especially when dictating an address over the telephone.

Naturally, the fact that the words must be spelled in groups of three (the proverbial English sandwich of consonant/vowel/consonant) relies heavily on their previous Rhythm lessons. Listening to and reading out the words and letters in a three-beat rhythm is essential.

The Vocabulary section that they have already passed through is now also well to the fore, as words that they may not understand are being introduced and entered into their vocabulary cache. It would be impossible to hold vocal spelling lessons without the students making use of their Speaking ability. If the words are read by different students and then written down, then the Reading and Writing areas, too, have been covered.

When starting any new section, all previous sections must be touched upon in sequence. This is the natural spiral of learning.

Dictation

After Spelling, Dictation comes automatically to mind. This is easily taught by recording your own voice into a recorder or a computer and allowing the students to access it and hear it again and again as often as is necessary. Real-time dictation from the teacher puts a time pressure on students that is not natural. In everyday language, if you do not hear exactly what someone says, you simply interrupt them and seek clarification. This is natural and often necessary. It is wrong and extremely foolish to presume that the person will say it once, and once only, at a speed that they dictate and over which you have no control. For this reason, Dictation is best recorded and not dictated.

Most teachers are forced by cash restraints, space restraints, or simply by their own laziness to teach Dictation by dictating passages to students. It always amazes me how often teachers object, and quite strongly, to my telling them that they are being lazy. They are equally amazed when I tell them that we are all lazy. Being a worker—and as a paid teacher you are simply a worker—it is natural to want to receive the highest amount of money for the smallest amount of time. There is nothing wrong with that. Employers, on the other hand, want to receive the maximum amount of time and effort for the smallest amount of money. This is natural and there is nothing wrong with that. Provided both employer and employee agree, then all are happy.

Dictation, whether dictated by the teacher to the whole class or to individual students by use of computer or recorders, must always be interesting. There are many books available which have pages and pages of graded passages for student dictation—a dream for the lazy teacher. The problem is that laziness has a cost. Use whatever time or energy you can spare to the choice of passages. "The tramp had cramp . . . " is a typical example of a simple dictation passage, but it is totally uninteresting to the students. Warning! If the passages are uninteresting, the teacher's work will be doubled. Secure interesting passages for your class, and you will save yourself much time and effort, with spectacular results to boot. Books such as Dr Seuss's *The Cat in the Hat* make dictation easy and so much more fun. Who can resist *Green Eggs and Ham*?

Dictating to the class as a whole has one advantage that should be milked. If dictation must be speeded up because some students are waiting or the end of the lesson is approaching, then the fact that the teacher will say the phrases three times and "three times only" should be emphasized and expanded upon. I teach the students that when listening to someone in normal everyday conversation, they may ask for clarity three times and no more. Japanese students feel quite comfortable asking four times, but the native English speaker will have none of it. Three strikes and you are out!

Interpretation

After dictation, the area that naturally follows is Interpretation. Here, the teacher must take great care. Interpretation varies greatly from normal speech—and this is the problem. Most students of English as a foreign language have studied passages with a view to answering the questions that follow. This in itself is fine, but the students then try to use this same format in speech, and this will not do.

Consider the following examples:

Table #19

Did the boy throw the stone?

Conversation: "Yes. He was a bad little tyke."

Interpretation: Yes. The boy threw the stone.

If these situations are reversed, problems arise.

Did the boy throw the stone?

Conversation: "Yes. The boy threw the stone." End of conversation!

Interpretation: Yes. He was a bad little tyke.

Teacher: "Just answer the question."

Native speakers do not normally attempt interpretation passages until they are ten years old or more. By that time, they are totally fluent in the language. They are native speakers. For students of English as a foreign language, to attempt interpretation passages while their spoken English is poor is a recipe for disaster.

Nonetheless, as teachers employed by schools, we must bow to the dictates of the establishment. This is fair. We take their money; we must play the game their way. He who pays the piper calls the tune! We must find a way to teach interpretation while maintaining the spoken English level. The simplest way to do this is to read out the answers to the interpretation questions and the spoken answers at the same time. "Did the boy go to school by bus? The answer to this is, 'Yes, the boy went to school by bus'—BUT if speaking, you would need to say, 'Yes. He was too tired to walk' or 'Yes. He had some money left' or something similar." The teacher should encourage the students to offer an original answer, the funnier the better. Only one volunteer answer is needed. Time constraints demand that almost no time be spent on this part of the lesson but the students so enjoy it that they often offer answers quickly. If no answer is forthcoming immediately, move swiftly onto the next interpretation question.

When the students realize that you are not going to wait for an answer they feel the need to provide one quickly. The fact that you are not waiting for them and that you are not concerned whether or not you receive an answer takes the pressure off the students, and they feel it's easier to answer. No matter whether they answer or not, you will have taught them that written English does not equal spoken English

Interpretation is the point where native English speakers and EFL speakers diverge. The native speaker is studying interpretation so that he may go on and study English literature. The EFL speakers may also go on to study English literature, but for them interpretation is a necessary practice for the time when they will have to translate English into their own language. For them, interpretation is really a practice exercise for when they have to look at a piece of written English and milk some meaning out of it. Extraordinary though it may seem, I have seen many examples of Interpretation taught as a practice exercise where students are given set questions and they must search the passage to find the answers. Most teachers know that this is but an exercise for the day when they will have a passage of English from which to wrestle some sense with no friendly teacher providing questions to lead the way. Despite this, I have never seen any teachers teach the students *how* to extract the meaning from an English passage. Most times, there seems to be an almighty leap from Interpretation to Translation. Before students can translate a passage into their own language, they must first of all milk the meaning and the feelings of the author from the passage. If they must do this, then it follows that they should be taught how to do it.

I once had a student whose English was excellent. She came for English lessons simply to keep her English polished and would occasionally bring in some piece of English that she had been given to translate. One day, she brought in a passage which was giving her some grief. I asked her to tell me what she had done so far so that I could see where she was going wrong. It was immediately obvious. She had been attacking the English from the front—i.e., the beginning—and in trying to work her way to the end had become bogged down in the grammar (which, in this particular piece of English, was ponderous). English sentence construction, unlike that of Japanese, is best attacked from the rear. I showed her that by working from the end of the passage to the front of the passage, the meaning became clear. To help her I gave her the following passage.

Table #20

"THANK YOU, JAPAN"

Washington is the capital of the United States. In Washington there are many wide streets and fine buildings. There are many fine parks, too. (*New Progress in English Book 2* by Robert M. Flynn)

By using only the first paragraph of "Thank You, Japan" as shown above, I showed her that in English it is easier to start at the end, as it is the last word in the sentence that is most important. I then asked her to mark out this word in the first sentence of the example. She appeared to think that this was boring; however, she marked the word *States*. "Ah!" I yelped. "You are starting at the beginning of the passage, and so you are heading into difficulty. The last word in the last sentence is *too*. It has a comma before it, and so the writer has given this word great emphasis. The rule is three beats to the comma and three beats to the period. That is how our notation works, and that is how our English language works."

She was now nodding in approval. I felt as though she were the teacher and I the student, and that I had just passed some kind of test in her eyes. I went on to explain further. "The *too* needs to be marked as a most important #3 word, as a #2 important word, and as a fairly important word. And remember that each part of that word then carries an equal amount of weight as all the other words so marked."

The next #3 word, *parks*, she managed well, but stumbled on which word should be #2. "Remember. Always ask yourself what this sentence is telling you about the word parks. It is telling you that there are many and that they are fine. The three words are therefore *many*, *fine* and *parks*." She could see that easily.

The next sentence showed very clearly another rule that she needed to learn. Words such as *and* or *but* almost always need a #2 mark of importance. Think of the simple sentences "A and B" or "A but B." Both of these sentences show the need for a rhythm giving equal emphasis to the conjunction no matter how lengthy and involved A or B might be.

She nodded happily and marked the passage thus:-

Table 20a

Washington is the <u>capital</u> of the United **States**. In Washington there are many wide *streets* <u>and</u> fine **buildings**. There are *many* <u>fine</u> **parks**, t<u>o</u>o.

She positively glowed when I pointed out to her that there twenty-four words in the paragraph above but only sixteen marked words and so if all of these words yet only these words are caught or explained by a dictionary, all of the other words are almost irrelevant. Mathematically speaking, that is only 66 percent of the paragraph.

Table 20b

Washington	capital	States
Streets	and	buildings
Many	fine	parks
to...................oo..................oo		

She was ecstatic. She could hardly believe that the meaning was actually clearer.

"Oh, I have better news than that," I boasted. "With only the last words, marked in bold, the sense is even better, and there are only four of them, making up just 16 percent approximately." She raced through the rest of the passage.

Table 20c

Washington is the capital of the United **States**. In Washington there are many wide *streets* and fine **buildings**. There are *many* fine **parks**, too.

One of the *finest* parks in Washington is Potomac **Park**. It is *on* the Potomac **River**. Every *spring* there is a big festival in this park. They call it the *Cherry* Blossom **Festival**. There are *3000* cherry trees **there**. Early in April it becomes *warm* and all these trees begin to **bloom**. How *beautiful* they **are!** How *pleasant* the park becomes!

Where did the cherry trees come **from?** They *came* from Japan! They are a *Japanese* gift to **America**. About 80 years *ago* the mayor of **Tokyo**, the capital of **Japan**, *sent* the capital of America all these cherry **trees**. He *wanted* to promote friendship between Japan and the **U.S.** What a *wonderful gift* it **was!** How *beautiful* it made the **city!**

Every *spring* many many people come to **Washington**. They *look* at the many fine **buildings**. They *walk* through the

133

beautiful parks. They *walk* by the Potomac *River* <u>and</u> go to Potomac **Park**. They want to *see* the Cherry <u>Blossom</u> **Festival**. There they *look* at all the beautiful cherry <u>blossoms</u> and they **say**, "T<u>ha</u>nk **you,** *Jap*<u>a</u>**n!**"

"Now comes the crucial part," I said. "If you had been given this passage to translate, following the rule that I have told you, how would you proceed?"

She was all smiles. "With 'Thank You, Japan.'"

"And then?"

"*Look, blossoms, say?*"

"Boo!" I mimicked the "out" button of a game show. "Go to the end of the next paragraph." That gives us:

Table 20d

Washington <u>capital</u> **States.** *streets* <u>and</u> fine **buildings.** *many* <u>fine</u> **parks,** t<u>oo</u>.

finest <u>Potomac</u> **Park.** *on* <u>Potomac</u> **River.** *spring* <u>festival</u> **park.**

Cherry <u>Blossom</u> **Festival.** 3000 <u>trees</u> **there.** *warm* <u>trees</u> **bloom.**

beautiful <u>they</u> **are!** *pleasant* <u>park</u> **becomes!**

Where <u>trees</u> **from?** *came* <u>from</u> **Japan!** *Japanese* <u>gift</u> **America.**

ago <u>mayor</u> **Tokyo,** *capital* <u>capital</u> **Japan,** *sent* <u>America</u> **trees.** *wanted* <u>friendship</u> **U.S.**

wonderful gift was! *beautiful* <u>made</u> **city!**

spring <u>people</u> **Washington.** *look* <u>fine</u> **buildings.**

Walk <u>through</u> **parks.** *River* <u>and</u> **Park.** *see* <u>Blossom</u> **Festival.**

look <u>blossoms</u> **say,** "T<u>ha</u>nk **you,** *Jap*<u>a</u>**n!**"

She jumped up and shook my hand. I smiled broadly at the praise echoing from her next words—"I'll come for English lessons from you on a weekly basis"—but my smile was made brighter by the financial aspect of the promise.

Never lose sight of the fact that teachers teach for money. Never fool yourself into thinking that you teach for the love of it. The love you experience from a job well done and the love that you earn from grateful students is but the icing on the gingerbread. If you think that you teach for the love of it, then think of earning the love of your employer. If you recognise that you teach for money, then make sure that you earn it. Remember: you are the expert. Check everything that you do and everything that you teach.

The rule of three is the very essence of the "Thank You, Japan" passage. Japanese people speak and think in fours while English-speaking people process everything in threes. Hence, even in grammar, we think of Subject, Verb, Object—SVO. Japanese students, to a man, interpret English grammar as SVOC or SVOO—Subject, Verb, Object, Complement or Subject, Verb, Object, Object. Instead of working against this fact, it is good for teachers to make use of it. Students who find it difficult to remember SVOC or SVOO will remember it quite easily when it is pointed out to them that native speakers do not bother about it. It is not the fact that they now have a smaller thing to remember that helps them to remember it. It is the fact that it is interesting and that they want to tell someone else about it that helps them to remember their own SVOC or SVOO method.

Japanese students seem to love grammar. Whether they love it because they are good at it or are good at it because they love i, is quite beyond me, and I have never sought to investigate the whys and the wherefores of this situation, but I make good use of it. They also very much appreciate tips that will help when the grammar is difficult to grasp. The "one s" rule is a good example of this.

Table #21

teacher talk	the teachers talk	or	the teacher talks
boy sing	the boys sing	or	the boy sings
girl walk	the girls walk	or	the girls walk
dog bark	the dogs bark	or	the dog barks

In the above examples, there is always only one "s" used at either the subject or the verb but not at both even when the sentence is in the question form.

Table #22

Do teacher talk?	Do the teachers talk?	or	Does the teacher talk?
Do boy sing?	Do the boys sing?	or	Does the boy sing?
Do girl walk?	Do the girls walk?	or	Does the girl walk?
Do dog bark?	Do the dogs bark?	or	Does the dog bark?

Again, only one "s" is used either at the first word or at the noun. The students never quibble with the fact that when the "s" is used at the word *do*, it requires an "e." If the basic rule works, the Japanese student will quite happily accept modifications or exceptions to it. The beauty of this rule is that the student thinks that he has only to insert an "s" and he has a 50 percent chance of being correct. The hidden benefit, of course, is that the teacher can use the method to introduce many verbs to the students, thereby incorporating a Vocabulary lesson into the Grammar lesson.

Although Japanese students have a tremendous amount of knowledge of grammar, they have often learned it out of context. Doing so enables them to learn a great amount in a short time but makes it very difficult to use later especially in spoken English. Phrases such as "hotter than," "taller than," "as good as," as cheap as," are better learned as "summer is hotter than winter," "He is taller than I," "He is as good as she is," "The coat is as cheap as the jacket." Using other students in the class makes the sentences even easier to remember.

One student I had once said, "I am more intelligent than Mei." Mei never let him forget it. Indeed, the whole class ribbed him about it for weeks. Months later, I found that almost everything that had been taught at that lesson had been well-remembered. That one incident had given the lesson a mental hook on which the students were able to hang everything.

Many, many moons ago, I similarly chanted my way through French grammar. At that time, in an attempt to remember which verbs carried which prepositions, we were given a list of verbs with the correct preposition beside it. They were difficult to remember. One teacher we had, made it easy for us. She made us chant things such as *"dire a quelq'un de faire quelque chose."* Over forty years later, I can still remember her lessons! The point here that I wish to stress is that the grammatical points were not learned in isolation but always as part of a sentence. The teacher whose lessons I still remember, had made them into interesting sentences. Learning grammar relies heavily on memory. Anything that relies so much on memory is perforce easily forgotten.

If a grammatical point can be explained as a logical conclusion of our way of thinking, it is so much the better. Students are always fascinated by the different ways in which foreigners think in comparison to themselves. To my students, one of the most amazing things is that their English conversation teachers—i.e., the native speakers—often know less grammar than they do. In these cases, I take great pains to explain that native English speakers often know very little about grammar. Indeed, a friend of mine who is not particularly intelligent and so not very well educated comes from a good family and speaks very good English but has difficulty in distinguishing between a noun and a verb, far less anything else. Another friend is a brilliant, well-educated mathematician specializing in electronics. He simply laughs if asked any question on grammar. He maintains that he left grammar behind with his toy soldiers.

Why, then, does the native speaker pay so little attention to grammar? It is because spoken English is better thought of more as an emotional language than a grammatical one. In Japanese, there is a subtle shift of language depending on the social status of the listener to that of the speaker. In English, the change is brought about by the degree of feeling existing between the two speakers. It is not a clear and distinct classification and it does not lend itself to the written word.

Conjugation

Many mental backs are broken when teachers decide to teach conjugation. How many children remember conjugating their way through *sleep, slept, was sleeping, had slept*, etc.? It has never failed to confuse me as to why this method was instigated in the first place.

The very young native English speaker and the no-so-young second-language learner have all been guilty of sticking "ed" onto the end of every and any verb.

All the language learners whether L1 or L2 are struggling to construct their own rules of grammar, called "interlanguage," even to the extent where they do not apply. Since the same error appears regardless of L1 or L2, we can conclude this is not triggered interlingually . . . (*English Language Education in Japan* - Hideo Oka - July 2010)

A child saying "teached" is not imitating and is not being ungrammatical. He is inventing and in a highly grammatical way. He is not saying "teached" because he heard someone else say it; he probably never did. He is saying it because he knows- though he could not put his knowledge into words- that other verbs form their past tense by adding the suffix-ed, and he therefore supposes that the verb "teach" should behave in the same way. This is in every way a reasonable assumption and a first class piece of thinking. All the more reason why we should meet such "mistakes," not with a curt correction, but with understanding and courtesy. (*How Children Learn* by John Holt)

This is so true, and naturally, a good teacher would never dream of correcting a student who has made such a mistake, other than with understanding and courtesy. It can be done with understanding and courtesy, while still being curt but kind.

With the very young or the very new learner of English, it does not matter in the slightest if they use the suffix "-ed." We will understand. It is, therefore, not essential to correct them every single time. If a quick interruption can be made, well and good; if not, simply waiting to the end of the pronouncement and reiterating the sentence with the correct verb format is normally enough. If not, a fun method of practicing the verb must be found. A method that is interesting produces much better results. If the method is boring, the students will give only half of their brain to the job on hand. Even good students will find themselves mentally straying from the path.

Adult students are the worst. I vividly remember, halfway through a boring lecture, suddenly wondering if I had enough vegetables at home for the dinner and realizing that I had been going through many items on my mental "to do" list for quite some time. I had been mentally dozing. I had not wanted to do such a thing. I had voluntarily attended the lecture and had desperately wanted to have the information that was being imparted. I was shocked at the bad behaviour of my brain. If such a thing can happen to an adult student wishing to learn, how much more likely is it in the young student who is there simply because his parents told him to attend?

Instinctively, every student knows when he is being subjected to bad teaching. A sure method of judging bad teaching is the length of time that the lesson seems to take. A good teacher teaching a good lesson is finished before the student realizes that the time is up. In a bad lesson, every student is painfully aware of the passing of time. So is the teacher!

Another part of the reason why many grammar lessons are so boring is the fact that they are not natural. Teaching material that is not natural instantly triggers a "Why am I learning this?" response from the students. When the teaching is bad, this type of response is felt no matter what subject is being taught. Learning verb conjugations as part of a *sleep/slept/was sleeping/had slept/had been sleeping* list may seem to be a quick way to teach many conjugations, but the amount of information lost as the students tune out the teacher, throws doubt on the efficiency of the method.

A far more effective method is to ask the students to make a list of five verbs. I always choose five verbs, no more. It is very tempting for teachers to ask the students to do more. No matter how often I have taught teachers this method there is always one teacher who asks the students to choose ten verbs. Ten is too many. There is a "not much" feel to having to do five things, and it is this feeling which is making the teacher choose ten verbs. The feeling from "ten" is rounded, is sufficient, is enough. Unfortunately, the student feels this too.

Ask the students to choose five verbs. Here is the fail-safe part of the exercise. I have never had a student fail at this. Even nursery school children who do not know what a verb is can give me five verbs if I ask them for five words for doing something. They see this as a simple task, and so they do it easily. The hidden joy in this for the teacher is that in a class of fifteen students, while there will be duplications, the students choose more than ten verbs between them—many more! The bigger the class, the more verbs will be chosen. The greater the class, the greater the duplication, but a greater number of verbs will be chosen.

The teacher then asks one student for his list of verbs and puts them on display for all to see. The exercise is now off to a confident and interesting start. The student who chose the words is all eyes and ears. They are his words. The others are interested in what he chose. Words chosen by the teacher never have this appeal. The teacher then chooses the English pattern that she wants to practice, and the students are asked to say five sentences about that particular student by using the five verbs in the list. "Yesterday, Yasu slept until

10:00 a.m. He ate at 1:00 p.m. He drank a Coca-Cola. He telephoned his friend. He went out." For more advanced classes the verbs can be linked together. "Yesterday, Yasu had been eating his lunch, and as he was drinking his Coca-Cola, he remembered something and telephoned his friend. That done, he went out." Because the sentences are about someone in the class, the lesson is interesting, and the students are keen to volunteer information. Even with advanced classes, this works. I have also used it successfully with adults.

When the students have to write the lesson, it is even better, as their ideas are often a little more fanciful. Students are keen to write about each other. They are not so keen to write about themselves. They are even less keen to write out verb conjugations apropos nothing. The first method produces great retention; the final method produces very little. A list of verb tenses such as *buy/bought/was buying* has little in it to help the student remember them. But if someone wrote that John bought a pink ribbon for his friend, the fact that John has a female friend and that he bought a pink ribbon for her are hooks for the mind to use for the word *bought*, and so retention is much greater. The mind loves interesting detail. More information, not less, is often the means of ensuring retention.

The final bonus in this type of teaching is that, come test time, if one of the questions happens to mention a pink ribbon or some other interesting detail that was mentioned in the lesson, the students will immediately recall the entire lesson. The brain is programmed to forget pain and suffering but remember pleasant times, and it will often recall them simply to relive the pleasure. Teachers should capitalize on this.

142

Many teachers blame the fact that they must teach so students pass tests to be the reason they must teach these harsh, boring lessons. This is blatantly untrue. The more retention, required the more the lessons must be interesting.

"Children start learning English in junior high school with great enthusiasm, but after a year or two, more than half of them begin to dislike English" (*English Language Education in Japan* - Hideo Oka - July 2010). How true this is! My own husband hated English while he was at school, and yet we now use English at home on a daily basis. We converse in it and we fight in it. His lack of English has never given me an edge in any of our heated discussions, and his lack of grammar has had absolutely no impact on either him telling me exactly what he thought or on my ability to understand what he was trying to say.

Grammar is taught ferociously in Japan. Here are some quotes from Hideo Oka on the state of English Teaching in Japan as of 2010 from *English Language Education in Japan*:

1)   There can be no doubt that many teachers favour grammar-translation because they themselves are the product of such teaching and as such do not feel comfortable communicating in English. In their view, studying grammar and vocabulary is synonymous with language learning, which is best achieved by detailed explanation and a great deal of memorization.

2)   Teachers of English usually blame university entrance examinations for forcing them to rely on the grammar-translation method.

3)   Without any pre-existing foundation in grammar and vocabulary, it would take them much longer

to master English, or they might not be able to achieve such a degree of accuracy.

4) Another stunning aspect of English teaching in Japan is the old-fashioned grammar-translation method. It is so prevalent that the target language is hardly used in class, except for reading aloud from an English textbook.

5) The gradation of teaching materials is implicitly grammar-based. As a result the passive voice is almost always taught in the 2nd yr of junior high school. As for the subjunctive mood, it is put off until senior high school because it is considered the most complex in conventional school grammar, an interpretation that completely disregards the important socio-linguistic role of the subjunctive in polite conversation (e.g. Would you like to have some tea?)

6) The general English courses were originally expected to teach integrated skills, but in reality teachers relied too heavily on reading and translation. That is why it was deemed necessary to establish Oral Communication courses at the sacrifice of grammar in 1994.

7) Paradoxically though, many teachers remain persistently biased towards the importance of grammar.

8) Although Grammar has disappeared from the Course of Study in theory, in actuality it is still taught in disguise during Oral Communication (OC) classes.

9) In these classes, a supplementary grammar book is often adopted and grammatical rules

are explained and practiced in a conventional manner, just like mathematical formulas.

10) . . . senior high school teachers complain that students enter higher education without a solid background of grammar or vocabulary.

11) . . . .it is not enough for our future teaching methods to be grammar-translation alone, nor just communicative alone. What is most urgently needed is to seek the best combination of learning and acquisition in formal instruction.

This then is where you—the expert, the native English speaker—come into play. Grammar in any country is only taught in schools long after the children have become proficient in their own spoken language. You, the expert, need to give them the necessary base on which they can later build a knowledge of grammar.

This type of English education cannot begin too early. Babies from birth make language one of their prime targets. Babies born into bilingual or multi-lingual households hear two or more languages from birth. "'The earlier, the better' may be true as far as pronunciation is concerned, but in the areas of grammar and vocabulary, it does not necessarily apply" (*English Language Education in Japan* – Hideo Oka – July 2010). In some ways this is true. Learning grammar as grammar belongs to a later stage in a child's education, but a strong base in spoken grammar can only be an advantage when that time comes.

In a survey we conducted with over 7,000 Japanese engaged in international businesses, it turned out that in spite of very high scores in the TOEIC (Test of English for International Communication) tests, they still found it difficult to make convincing presentations or to negotiate to their advantage (Koike, 2008). (*English Language Education in Japan* – Hideo Oka – July 2010)

This is natural and lends credence to the need for native speakers to help students speak English.

There are a number of public tests of English proficiency. . . . The best known of these tests is the Eiken English proficiency test, which emulates the formal ELE . . . . The TOEIC (Test of English for International Communication) is aimed at business people, while the TOEFL (Test of English as a Foreign Language) targets those who wish to study at universities abroad. (*English Language Education in Japan* – Hideo Oka – July 2010)

None of these tests aim to test the speaking ability of the student. I have seen some such tests brought to me by my students, and I would have difficulty trying to pass some of them. They are aimed at EFL students and not native speakers. If we are to teach students to speak and to understand spoken English, we need native English speaking experts.

Where

There are English conversation schools dotted all over every large town in Japan. These "schools" are called English Conversation schools to differentiate between English as taught in educational establishments, loaded with grammar. The anomaly is that despite a considerable rise in the number of English Conversation schools and the fact that English is now featured in compulsory education, there has not been a considerable rise in the English conversation ability of the average student. There are many reasons.

English Conversation Schools

Most of these are run purely for business reasons; nonetheless, they do offer students a place, usually fairly nearby their office or station, where they can meet and converse with foreigners. The problem is that this will not improve their conversation skills very much, as most students will simply be practicing their own mistakes. The teacher turnover in most of these establishments is fairly high, and this poses another problem. However, the greatest problem of all is that there is no educational scheme for teachers to follow, and most teachers are left to their own devices, thereby ensuring that there is no teaching being done.

Classroom Conditions

Many teachers of English language employed in schools complain about the teaching conditions. This is natural. There are no such thing as ideal conditions. There are only bad teaching conditions and terrible teaching conditions. It is simply a fact, and teachers must continue to teach despite them.

> These days, the number of students in an English class is limited to 40- but even that number astounds foreign language teachers because such a large class size makes it all but impossible to teach a modern language effectively. (*English Language Education* in Japan - Hideo Oka - July 2010)

This is a song sung so often by foreign teachers in Japan. It is, however, simply not true. As a Scottish teacher, who has taught in Scotland (where the population in 2012 was less than six million), I often taught to classes of ten or twelve children. Japanese people nod wisely when I tell them this, but then their eyes open wide in surprise when I explain that the children in the class were aged from four to thirteen years of age because that class was actually the entire school.

In Fukuyama, at Tenshi Nursery, I regularly taught three classes in a morning with each class having more than eighty children in it. Indeed, the youngest class had over ninety children. The level of English in each class rises perceptibly each time, but with my amount of experience this is no great feat; indeed, would be shameful if it were otherwise. In Osaka, at Tsukamoto Nursery, one of my teachers, a twenty-three-year-old lad, young but well-trained in methodology, taught a weekly class of sixty children.

I have often been asked what the ideal size is for a class. This is a question too difficult for me. Suffice it to say that the smaller the class the more difficult it is to teach, and the larger the class the more difficult it is to keep control. One is an educational problem and the other is a discipline problem. Teachers well trained in the art of teaching can teach either.

Students who insist on a one-student class give themselves tremendous problems. I refuse to teach "man-to-man." Despite my teaching credentials and my many years of teaching, I find it far too difficult to ensure sure and swift progress through the lesson aims if there is only one student in the class. The first difficulty is that repetitive drills are reduced to once or twice instead of the ten or twenty times carried out in a larger class, and the student is unable to learn from the mistakes of others. This loss of discovery is crucial. In a one-student class, there are no others. A one-student class will often decline into conversation between the teacher and student, with the result that the student is simply practicing and entrenching his own mistakes. The aim for the lesson is often lost in the process. The greatest difficulty in teaching a one-student class is that the student is always the focus of the teacher's attention. The student is always on stage in a one student class. There is no time to relax and conjugate what he has learned.

The number of students in a class is important; however, the greatest problem in teaching is not the size of the class but the size of the classroom. Too few children in a huge hall is difficult, and too many children in a small space is all but impossible. In schools, the situation is almost always close to ideal. There, the sizes of the classes almost always match the sizes of classrooms.

"Learning English as a school subject officially begins at the age of 12. . . . According to the Course of Study, there must be a minimum of 315 hours of English instruction in junior high school" (*English Language Education in Japan* – Hideo Oka – July 2010). In senior high school, the number of hours varies.

> According to the Course of Study. . . In Senior high school the number of hours varies between 400 and 450. Depending on the curriculum adopted by a particular school, students receive 4-6 periods of English instruction per week over a three year period, Inasmuch as over 90 percent of Japanese students complete high school, it can be said that almost everyone in Japan studies English for at least six years.
>
> In the year 2000, as many as 49.1 percent of high school graduates moved on to attend a university or college, where students generally have two 90-minute periods per week. . . . The total number of hours of English instruction during eight years of formal schooling thus comes to well over 800 hours. Even so, most students never develop any confidence in their English ability. The reasons for this dismal result are manifold, but the way English is taught in classrooms all over the country is a major contributing factor. (*English Language Education in Japan* – Hideo Oka – July 2010)

Oka tells us that, officially, children in junior secondary schools have English taught to them as a single category with no subdivision. When they reach senior secondary school, they have two hours of oral communication, and in the third year, they have a four-hour course of reading. By the time the children graduate from senior secondary, they will have no more than 2,700 words. He points out that a few decades previously they needed 3,500 words. This would seem to herald a decline in ability. Oka also gives us some facts about the use of native English speakers.

> In order to improve the ELE situation, the Japan Exchange & Teaching (JET) program was introduced in 1987. As of 2001, there were 6190 foreign university graduates working as assistant teachers in language classes in Japan, mostly teaching English (about 5 percent of foreigners from non-English speaking countries are invited to teach other languages). (*English Language Education in Japan* - Hideo Oka - July 2010)

English is taught in schools and universities, and it can be said that the amount being taught is ideal. It gives students sixteen or seventeen years of English.

Although school classrooms provide teachers with excellent situations in which to teach, there are some inherent problems when teaching in schools. One of these problems is the rush, or the force, on teachers and student alike as the pressure is applied to ensure that the students pass the relevant examinations. "Japanese children's school careers are punctuated at various stages by the necessity to take entrance examinations. For some of them the infamous 'examination hell' begins in the final two years of elementary school" (*English Language Education* in Japan - Hideo Oka - July 2010)

There is little chance for the teacher, the native speaker, the expert, to indulge in some explorative investigation of the language. To earn your salary, you must teach as best you can. Yet do so may be to do a disservice to the students who, for their approaching examinations, must learn grammatically based English as fast as they can with no time allowed for correction of the peculiarities that often occur. The result is pidgin English. This resultant type of pidgin English is often referred to as Japlish. This problem can easily be overcome if care is taken by the native speaker, the expert, to ensure that all teaching material is scrutinized before the session begins and that only natural, native English is spoken to the students.

I once attended a prestigious Japanese school as one of a party of six English speakers to test the Spoken English of the students in the classes. A group of us gathered together prior to the test and we chatted as we waited. Despite the fact that we chatted for more than ten minutes, I did not learn the names of the other testers, nor they mine.

When we were all seated in the test area, at quite a distance from each other, I was greeted by my first group of students. "Hello. Nice to meet you," they all chanted in unison.

As a teacher, I was appalled. These children had been taught by native speakers, and yet, had I, as a teacher standing in my own classroom, been greeted by native English-speaking children with "Hello," they would have been well and truly reprimanded for their bad manners. However, I decided that as I was hired to test their English and not their manners it would be better to ignore it. I simply replied with, "Good afternoon."

The first question from them, however, could not be ignored. "What's your name?" one of them asked.

I explained that I was a teacher and that teachers and old ladies do not like to be asked that question. They were understandably puzzled. They had been taught—by native English speakers—to ask this question.

At that moment, I clearly heard another set of children speaking to one of the other testers, a man with whom I had just chatted upstairs. "What's your name?" came clearly from that other group.

Just as clearly came the over-enunciated reply: "My . . . name . . . is . . . Geoffrey . . . Hunter."

I cannot understand what makes people lose all sight of their own language when put into the position of speaking it in a teaching situation. I decided to do something about it. When we finished and went back upstairs, I turned to the man and said, "Sorry. I don't know your name."

He replied, "Geoffrey. Just call me Jeff." No sign of any, "My . . . name . . . is . . . "

Although the English being taught in this scenario was poor, the idea was good. The situation was an interactive one. Children of primary-school age are very active in everything they do and take an active interest in new things. Apparently, this interest in the language does not last.

In their first year or so, junior high school students are still active in class and may even volunteer to answer. By the second or third year, when they reach adolescence, their eagerness has usually waned and the teacher has to call up the students by name to elicit any answer at all. (*English Language Education in Japan* - Hideo Oka - July 2010)

Some junior high school students may still take an active interest, but by senior high school, students have been learning English for six years and become uninterested.

"On the whole, university students are just as listless as high school students are" (*English Language Education in Japan* – Hideo Oka – July 2010).

Apparently in universities, audio-visual material is widely used. This is perfectly acceptable provided the audio-visual material is acceptable. You are the native speaker. You are the expert. Check it.

> The new curriculum guidelines for elementary schools were announced in March 2008 and attracted many people's attention. In particular, English was made mandatory in the 5th and 6th grades of elementary school. However, it is not a "regular" class subject, like Japanese or algebra, which are subject to numerical evaluations. It will be taught one hour a week as part of a "foreign language activities" class, to be formally enforced in 2011 across the nation. (*English Language Education in Japan* – Hideo Oka – July 2010)

It is often thought impossible for students to become fluent with only one lesson per week. This is not the case. I have many students who became fluent with only one hour of English per week. It does mean, however, that the teacher must be meticulous in what is planned, what is taught, and how it is taught. There certainly is no time for fooling around with funny English that needs to be eradicated and then replaced.

As the native speaker, as the expert, employed in schools, you must check everything that you are asked to teach. For the sake of the children, you must ensure that it is correct the first time. Never teach anything that you would not say to your mother, your teacher, or the man next to you in a bar. These are your checklists. Run everything through them.

Alternative Classrooms

Not all English as a foreign language is taught in schools. There is, unfortunately, no indication of the number of native English speakers who are teaching English in English conversation schools or privately from their own homes. There are also many native English speakers who meet their students by appointment in local cafés or bars and teach them there. This is good, but here, too, there are problems.

The first problem with private homes and cafés has already been addressed: this type of "lesson" is almost always not a lesson and so the students are simply engaging in conversation and reinforcing their own mistakes. You, the expert, should ensure that this does not happen.

I taught English in The Main Bar in Nishinomiya for the Japan Scotland Association. The students were members of the Japan Scotland society, and some of them had been speaking English and working abroad where they used English daily for many years. They all liked to go to Scotland often, and so one of the members, Shigenobu Namba, had made out a wonderful script for us to use as a textbook. It was based on travelling from Japan to Scotland and covered every piece of English that could be deemed necessary to ensure that the students were able to go to Scotland and be confident in their English ability to do so.

For the first lesson, I took along some basic English rules to explain how I intended to go about the teaching the class. At the first lesson, I took notes on what needed to be taught based on faults found in the previous lessons. I prepared lessons for the next class. The newcomers to English had no problems with the lessons whatsoever, but the members who had used English for ten and fifteen years had a shock. No one corrects an adult speaker, and so their errors had become ingrained. The result was that the better the student, the harder they found the lessons. They had to struggle to change methods of speaking that they had been using, without correction, for many, many years.

The other problem with private homes and cafés is that there is no surety that the student will have sixteen or seventeen consecutive years of teaching. If that is understood, this second problem is halved. One look at the expert teacher, the baby, would lead us to believe that the preferred classroom is the home. This is not the case. Most mothers take their babies outside regularly. Mostly they are taken to the supermarket while the mother does her shopping. In our nursery school, where the children enter with only Japanese ability but soon become bilingual, we try to ensure that there are sufficient outings to give the children a solid base for their English. One outing is, of course, to the supermarket.

The children are given a written shopping list and the older children read it out to the younger ones prior to setting off for the store. Once there we take them through the aisles talking all the time about what they have on their lists and where it can be found. One such outing resulted in a child talking about the vegetables.

"What do you call these?" he asked pointing to *eringe*.

"Mushrooms," I replied.

"Eh? What do you call these?" he then asked and pointed to some mushrooms.

"Mushrooms," I replied.

156

"Eh . . . ? What do you call these?" he asked pointing to some *matsutake.*

"Mushrooms," I replied.

Now the game was on. The children pointed to *shimeji, enokidake, bunashimeji, shiitake, maitake,* and *nameko,* each time asking what it was called. To each and every question, I replied simply, "Mushrooms." The children found this hilarious. The Japanese identify each type of mushroom by names known to every housewife and child, while to us, they are simply differing forms of mushrooms.

Shortly afterwards, we rounded a corner and came upon a huge display of shoes. This was unusual in this supermarket, and so it instantly caught the children's attention. "What do you call these?" asked another boy.

"Eh?" I gasped. This time it was I who was shocked. He knew the word for shoes very well. All the children know the word for shoes. In Japan, shoes are removed prior to entering houses, some shops, and even some bars. Naturally, in our nursery, the children remove their shoes before entering, place them in a shoe rack, and retrieve them and put them on again at the door prior to going home. Every day, the word *shoes* is heard, numerous times.

Before I had time to reply, every child, every single child, answered in unison, "Mushrooms."

It was a huge joke. Outnumbered, defeated, I simply replied, "Well I wouldn't like to cook or eat these." To the children, this was not as funny as their own joke.

Months later, two little girls were having a bit of a contretemps and I asked what was wrong. "She took my mushroom," said the smallest child. There was no food to be seen. I wondered about this but the other child, although slightly belligerent, was in full acceptance of the statement.

157

"Did you eat her mushroom?" I asked. Both children burst out laughing. All belligerence was gone. All anger was gone. I took that opportunity to look around. "Aha," I said. "Did you take her stool?"

The second child replied, "Mine was the pink one."

Both children knew what was being discussed, and it took me only two or three seconds to understand too. Children do not dither over a word. For them, any port in a storm, any word in an argument. "Don't chase the word. Get on with the story" (Elizabeth Moss – English, French and German speaker).

Another problem that teachers encounter when teaching in alternative classrooms, especially one's own home, is the lack of preparation time. In schools, there is always time in the staffroom, with all the tools of the trade lying around, to ensure that preparation can be done. Teaching at home tempts the teacher to have another cup of coffee prior to the arrival of the student, finish putting the final touches to the dinner, or whatever. Although teachers normally spend far too much time in preparation, doing none is foolhardy.

The final type of alternative classroom is an order-made type of room. This is ideal. In some ways, it is even better than the classroom. Teaching cooking in English, or teaching some other skill in a room dedicated to the skill being taught, is an excellent method of teaching a foreign language. But the same problem exists here, too. In such situations, language aims are often not planned nor even sought. This results in much casual language usage and is an excellent Listening lesson, but grammar is often sadly lacking—or worse, abused.

In summation, for the expert teacher, any classroom will suffice. You are a native speaker. You are an expert in your own language—but can you teach it?

Why

Why do people want to learn English?

There are as many reasons as there are people. Many would say that they want to learn English to make friends with English-speaking people. Perhaps some would say that they want to learn English in order to fight with English-speaking people, but surely they would be in the minority. This being the case then there is no need to teach students fighting English. In fact, we should guard against it.

Amazingly, many teachers of English as a second language teach fighting English to their students. Some teachers do it with a knowing disregard for the fact, but others do it without even being aware that they are doing it. Some teachers do not even know that there is such a thing as fighting English.

English is an Emotional Language

If you are interested in teaching English as a foreign language, then you should know that English is a very emotional language. English-speaking people are able, while maintaining a very bland countenance, to deliver a joke or a scathing comment by their clever choice of words. This is because English is an emotional language.

There are three major levels of emotion in English. One is used when the speaker has no feelings, another when he has mild feelings, and the third when he has strong feelings. These levels are further subdivided into like or dislike in the case of mild feelings, and into love and hate when the feelings are strong.

Table #9

No feeling	Mild feeling	Strong feeling
:	:	:
:	:	(4) Love
:	(2) Like	:
(1)	:	:
:	(3) Dislike	:
:	:	(5) Hate
:	:	:
:	:	:

"How do you do?"

Although this is a rather cold way to greet people, it is often the most appropriate. When we first meet someone, we may be predisposed to like or dislike them according to what we have heard about them, but if we meet someone for the first time, it is safe to assume that will have no feelings towards them, and so it is correct to say, "How do you do?" or "Pleased to meet you."

The first greeting, "How do you do?" carries no feelings at all. The second greeting has a slight warmth, but as often as not, "Pleased" is a polite lie. It carries a little feeling, but native speakers will often use it to convey this slight warmth of feeling, although they do not actually feel it. For this reason, some people prefer the slight falsehood in "Pleased to meet you" to the slight coldness in "How do you do?"

The alternatives are "Happy to meet you," and "Glad to meet you." Both of these greetings convey much more emotion. The word *happy* belongs to the mild feelings group and *glad* belongs to the strong feelings group. The students are able to understand it more easily if told that the word *pleased* sends the equivalent of a smile, the word *happy* sends the person a large grin, and the word *glad* sends a picture of you jumping up and down with delight.

To teach all of this to students who have a good grasp of English is fine, but to teach it to beginners would be rather silly. It would only confuse the student. This is where you, the native speaker, must use your expertise. Choose one suitable expression for your students, then ask yourself, "Would it work in a bar, in a classroom, in my house?" When you have decided on a greeting you consider appropriate, you must then consider an appropriate answer to teach.

"Fine, thank you. And you?"

Many students of English as a foreign language have learned to reply to "How do you do?" with "Fine, thank you. And you?" Before teaching this as an answer we must stop and consider whether it is appropriate or not. "How do you do?" is a rather cold greeting, and to teach the student to respond with a question that turns the cold greeting back on the speaker is not very wise. "Fine, thank you," would be sufficiently cool for a reply. It is also simple and safe.

I recommend teaching "How do you do?" if first to speak and "Fine, thank you" if cast in the role of responder. I prefer to teach the students to reply to "How do you do?" with "How do you do?" and I tell them to say it as soon as the first person begins to speak, resulting in both people speaking at once. If the introduction begins with speaker A then the student will hear, "How do you do?" The student should then immediately, and quickly, reply with the same question.

The introduction would then be:

A: How (B: *How do*) do you (B: *you do?*) do?

The benefits in this are that the student needs learn only one sentence instead of two; also, at an introduction, a conversation is not required, and so the question, "And you?" is annoying to the first speaker. Speaker A does not want to reply and therefore be drawn into a conversation, and yet to ignore the question would be rude. Once again, the student has been taught antagonistic English.

Every town, every country carries its own colloquialisms but these should never be taught to students of a foreign language. "G'day, mate," "Top o' the morning to you," "Fit like the day," or "How's it gohn Serra Bel?" are all equally inappropriate. Native speakers may speak in this manner, but they do not like to hear others doing it. Indeed, they often think that the non-native speaker is making a fool of them. It follows, then, that all of these expressions are, once again, examples of students being taught antagonistic English. At an introduction, the aim should be to make friends or at least to try not to make enemies. Do not teach your student to irritate native speakers.

Sometimes a student will have a need for a spontaneous greeting. Here, too, the aim is to promote friendship, not antagonism. What, then, should the student say when simply greeting someone without the benefit of a preliminary introduction?

"Hello."

Someone, somewhere, at some time, taught students of English as a foreign language to say, "Hello," and the rest of us have suffered since. As a teacher, I am not amused to be greeted by "Hello." As a member of the female gender and of sufficient years for my grey head to demand a modicum of respect, I am insulted by "Hello." Once again, the student has been taught fighting English. Any teacher, being a native speaker and running it through the bar, classroom, house scenarios, would soon have found it acceptable in the bar, unacceptable at home, and intolerable in the classroom. We can all imagine the teacher's face if a student came in and greeted her with, "Hello."

If anyone visiting us had gone out for a while and then on returning had greeted my mother with, "Hello," she would have asked if we thought that we were speaking to the cat's mother and then blasted us with "Hello? What? Do you mean, 'Hello. Have you been busy?' or 'Hello. We're home early today'?" "Hello. Something, something, something," is acceptable. But a mere "Hello," is a passport to a verbal dressing-down. Not a thing to teach young students. In a bar, it works because people in bars do not need much in the way of respect to each other, and often any sense that was in the head of the person sitting there may have left an hour or so ago.

The students are understandably confused by all of this and so, as explained in one of the previous chapters, it helps if the student understands that "Hello" literally means "Is there any intelligent life form there?" This piece of English is universally taught by native speakers, and yet, it is so insulting. Not a good way to win friends and influence people.

"Good morning/afternoon/evening."

"Good morning," is a little distant and cool, but it is still good to teach older students. Younger children should stick to "Good morning," but older students and adults may use the more friendly, "Morning!" or "Afternoon!" or indeed "Evening!" if it be that time of day. Remember, you are the native speaker. You are the expert. Think it out before you teach it.

I have made a little book for my nursery school children that teaches "Hello Spot/Hello Stripey," for animals, "Morning, Thomas /Morning, James" for young lads, and "Good morning Mr. Adams" for addressing adults. This helps to show the differences in the greetings, but it is not essential. The children in our nursery soon become bilingual, and so it is necessary for them to learn the finer points of the language, but for the normal EFL student, "Morning," is simple and safe. Simple and safe should be the English teacher's motto. Do not teach the students to fight.

"My name is/I am . . . "

In a previous chapter, "What is your name?" "My name is . . ." and "I am . . . " have already been covered and dismissed as wrong and dangerous. The method of answering the question using the following format has also been covered: "John. John Smith,"(if one wants to be friends and be called John) or "Smith. John Smith,"(if one wants to keep a little distance and be called Mr. Smith).

When teaching this format, it is good, at this point, to explain to the students that they should never use Mr., Mrs., or Miss with their own name. It is necessary to explain to them when they may use Mr. and Mrs., and when they can use someone's Christian name. I am often extremely annoyed by young people using my Christian name when I have not granted them this privilege. Until they are deemed to be my friend they may not use it. Mr. and Mrs. means "I can never be your friend." When I am addressed in this manner, then it is up to me to say, "Call me Maud," thereby letting them know that I consider them to be a friend.

Students are always puzzled by this, until it is explained that in an office scenario, the cleaner will often come in and greet the boss with, "Good morning, Henry," and he will likely respond with "Morning, Mrs. Anderson." They realize that they have often seen this in films and wondered about it. They should be told that the cleaner is acknowledging the boss's position. By the using the full expression, "Good morning" she indicates that she is speaking up to him, but at the same time, the use of his first name indicates that she is happy to be friends with him whenever he wants. He, on the other hand, delivers a more distant greeting. The use of the clipped "Morning" indicates that he is talking down to someone or to no one in particular, as when a greeting to a room full of people, while indicating, by the use of the Mrs. Anderson, that he has no desire to ever be her friend. Neither of them is offended. It is as it should be.

Similarly, students should not use the abbreviation Ms. when talking to a woman. It can be written but it should never be spoken. I explain to them that most woman are not insulted by being addressed as Miss or as Mrs., but some are deeply offended if addressed as Ms., considering it to be an inhuman appellation. In America, it is more acceptable, but in many other countries, it certainly is not. Care should be taken with the use of Ms. The students are learning English to make friends. Insulting people, even if accidentally, will not promote friendship.

Asking for someone's name has been touched on in a previous chapter, but it is such a perfect way to make enemies that it bears being looked at once more. "What is your name?" (fit only for policemen) has been addressed but not yet fully investigated. A simple way to teach the asking of a name is to tell the students that we consider the giving of our name to be a privilege, almost a present. Remind students that if they give someone a birthday present, then they are likely to receive one when their own birthday comes around. If you want to know someone's name, give your own name. Few native speakers can resist giving their own name if someone says, "Hello. I'm John. John Smith." If the student wishes to find out someone's name without giving his or her own name, then he should use, "Sorry, I don't know your name." This, while indicating that friendship is not being sought, will almost certainly result in the name that the student wishes to hear being given. If a person so addressed replies with a refusal such as "Oh. That's okay," then there is no need to care about offensive English anymore. This person does not wish to be friends. However, such difficult phraseology need not be taught. By simply giving his or her own name, a student will undoubtedly solicit that of the other person without any offence being given.

"Where are you going?"

This will certainly not promote friendship. This is yet another horror of the English often taught to students of English as a foreign language. As the expert, as the native speaker, imagine a bar scenario whereby someone stands up and hears from the person sitting next to him, your student, "Where are you going?" The answer may not defy imagination, but it probably defies printing. In a classroom scenario, the teacher could well use this to a student but it is not likely to endear the teacher to the student. It may in fact instill fear. The imagination shrivels when trying to picture a student posing such a question to a teacher. In the house, a mother would certainly ask such a question to a child, and a child would almost certainly ask such a question of his mother. However, the question fails on two out of three. This is because this question implies that the person leaving is doing something strange. This will not promote friendship.

"Going somewhere nice?"

This is a much preferable way to solicit the information required. However, it is hard to imagine the reply to that from someone who was going to the toilet. Imagine the reply from someone who was going to order more drinks. Imagine the reply to that from any kind of scenario, and if it fails the test in even one kind of scenario, do not teach it. Your student does not need to learn how to pick a fight. If they are so inclined, they will manage well enough without your help.

It stands to reason then that one cannot ask where anyone is going. It often helps in such a situation, as when the student wants to know where a person is going to simply say, "Bye." The person who is on his way somewhere will almost always smile and say, "I'm only going to the toilet," or "I'll be back soon," or "Bye." All are safe. This English can then be taught.

Asking questions is difficult, but apologizing is even more so. In an apology, the inherent problem is that, far from antagonizing anyone the student is actually trying to smooth the vibes between himself and another person. Yet, so much of the English taught to the students is likely to inflame the situation rather than smooth it over.

"Excuse me."

Harmless though it may seem, this phrase is loaded with dynamite. Many native speakers do not know the grammatical rules behind some words, and they do not need to know any. If you are a native speaker, you are an expert. You can feel the hidden menace.

However, to aid the explanation it helps to look at the grammatical use here. Although "Excuse me" is technically present tense, imperative mood, it is best thought of as future tense and is used to signal that a bad thing is about to happen. It is therefore used as in, "Excuse me. Could you tell me the time?" or "Excuse me. Is this the way to Abbey Road?" The words "excuse me" are used to apologize before the inconvenience; ergo, the bad thing is about to happen and so it is viewed as future tense. On hearing these words, the listener stops and is prepared for some inconvenience. Imagine the student bumping someone in a bar and saying, "Excuse me." This is perhaps harder for the reader to understand than the previous examples, and so a good way of testing any words or phrases that seem doubtful and that seem to pass the bar, classroom, house scenarios is to imagine the answer that these words solicit.

Table #23

Speaker A:	Excuse me.
Speaker B:	Yes?
Speaker A:	Excuse me.
Speaker B:	What?
Speaker A:	Excuse me.
Speaker B:	What do you want?

All of these answers are possible, and all show some level of annoyance, even if only that shown by the first example. The speaker shows willingness to be disturbed, but the implication that he is about to be disturbed is there. Bumping into him and then implying that a further or a worse thing is about to happen could be downright dangerous. I have heard native speakers use "Excuse me" in these scenarios, but they have the correct body language that belies the incorrect use of the words, and so the offence is not so great. Students of English as a foreign language often still use their own native body language, many standing rigidly to attention, and so the offence is magnified.

"Pardon me."

"Pardon me" again technically present tense, imperative mood, it is best thought of as past tense and is used to signify that the bad thing for which the apology is being offered is in the past and will remain there. Things that have been granted a pardon are in the past, and it is always assumed that they will stay there. It is therefore unforgivable, extremely silly, and may even be downright dangerous for the student to use "pardon me" for something over which he has no control. Most students have no need for this type of apology.

"Sorry."

"Sorry" is almighty. "Sorry" is present tense. When "sorry" is said, the assumption is that the apology and the bad action are happening at one and the same time. Even when this is not the case, the native speaker will use "sorry" to imply that he wishes that it were so. Consider the following examples:

Student: Sorry I was absent last week.

Teacher: (Millions of replies are possible.)

Unless the student is a habitual absentee. I would be surprised if the teacher showed any annoyance. Although grammatically wrong because the offence took place last week and so technically "pardon me" would be a better choice, the use of "sorry" is more correct in that it uses the emotional aspect of the English language and asks that the event and the apology be considered as happening simultaneously. There is, therefore, no need to teach "Excuse me" or "Pardon me." "Sorry" is all that will ever be needed.

Why do you want to teach English?

Most people to whom I have addressed this question answer rather sheepishly that they see it as a quick and effective way to earn some ready cash to fund world travelling. This so annoys me. They need not be sheepish about it at all. It is indeed a quick and easy way for them to earn some cash, because they are highly qualified and therefore greatly desired as teachers of English as second language. As a native English speaker, you are an expert. All over the world, English language teaching schools will pay highly for such an expert. You need not feel ashamed of such work. You should be proud to be of help. You must, however, use all of your expertise.

Most teachers of English who are non-native speakers are normally highly qualified in the grammar of English and know much more than most native speakers on all the technical points. This is as it should be. These teachers, or schools, are not employing native speakers because of their technical ability. They are employing native speakers for two reasons, and both are related to their native speaking ability. They want to know if the native speaker can understand what the students are saying and whether the students can understand what the native speaker is saying to them. This is all they ask. However, if this is all you give then you are, in a way, short-changing them. They know no better, but you do. If they are teaching some horrendously offensive English and you feel this to be the case, offer them your advice. Show them where you feel it to be wrong. They will in all probability not want to know. That is their choice. You have done your part and can now cheerfully take the money offered with no feelings of guilt.

If enough people point out the same things, eventually someone will realize that English is an emotional language and that the students are learning how to fight with everyone. There is very little that can be done other than that. If you are hired to teach English from a book that

171

is full of nasty English, you would be a fool to refuse to use it. Firstly, you would probably lose the highly paid job, and even if you did not, you would antagonize the English teaching staff.

If you are hired to teach one of the classes where the English is at a higher level, then you may well be able to simply chat to the students to fully earn your salary. Normally, however, chatting is simply not good enough. Every teacher should teach a lesson. It need not be a heavy lesson full of writing and grammatical points. It may well be a chat type of lesson. Nonetheless, as the teacher, you should have an aim in mind before you start the lesson, and you should check whether or not your aim was met when you finish the lesson. Ideally, these aims are gleaned by you by observing the mistakes made by students in previous lessons. If in one of your lessons you noticed a student using "buyed" instead of "bought," and despite one correction of the point it happened again, then instead of continually correcting him to the point of boredom, it is better to simply take a memo and prepare a lesson on "bought" for the next time you teach that class. This is such a common mistake and one good lesson on it should eliminate the problem completely.

One of the simplest ways to ensure a good but very enjoyable lesson is to divide the class in half. One half of the class should be shopkeepers and the other half shoppers. The students tend to enjoy the lesson more when they choose the type of shop by themselves. The younger the class, the more physical the lesson needs to be, so children should draw two items for sale in their shop for the other children to buy. With older classes, the students can sit where they are and simply talk across the classroom to the shopkeeper of their choice. The most important part of the lesson is that you must tell them that once they *have bought* two items they are finished and that after they *have bought* one item they will have to wait a little before they can tell the others what they *have bought*. In this way, the aim of the lesson is laid out for all to see. When the students are shopping you should continually keep the aim in sight by asking the students if they had any difficulty when they bought the shirt or whatever item they bought. In this way, the aim has been introduced and taught. In order to consolidate it the students must be able to use it easily. This is done by asking the students to tell the others what they bought at what shop. The students should use the format, "I bought apples at the greengrocers and I bought a shirt at the drapers."

In this manner the students are using the "manual" part of their brains in order to teach themselves the names for the different shops, and so they are "automatically" learning the past tense of *buy* with no effort whatsoever. This use of the manual part of the brain while exploiting the automatic part of the brain is good teaching. The manual and the automatic parts of the brain are best explained by using a simple act such as walking or breathing. We breathe without thinking. This automatic breathing is extremely efficient. We can, however, take over and breathe manually, but when we concentrate on breathing, we do not do it so efficiently. Breathing becomes automatic immediately after birth, but some other tasks, such as walking, take longer. Talking takes even longer. This is the case with other tasks, and this turning of a manual task to an automatic one is a teacher's aim.

In primary school, the teacher taught us to add 2 plus 2. At that time it was a difficult manual task. Now the number 4 is in our brains without us even thinking about it. This is teaching at its best.

Many young native speakers employed for a year or two as EFL teachers object to the idea of having to fit in to patterns set by others. Unfortunately, this will always be the case. The full-time teacher has a plan stretching over several years to ensure that after a set period of time the students will have covered all the points they need to learn in order to speak the target language.

A non-native speaker learning English as a second language will normally take ten years to speak it perfectly. There are some who believe that it is impossible to become fluent with only one lesson per week. This is certainly the case if the lessons are not part of a whole and do not hinge upon each other. This should not happen. It is possible for students to become fluent with only one lesson per week if the lessons are well taught and form part of an overall plan. I have seen it happen too often to doubt it.

In the chapter headed "When," I have laid out a plan to ensure, provided the plan is followed meticulously and that lessons are well prepared and delivered, that students will become fluent after ten years. Most schools have such an overall plan, and to deviate from it is to ensure that the students have no chance of becoming fluent. This would be most unfair and almost dishonest. Offer advice whenever you see bad English being taught, but do not deviate from the overall plan without thought as to the consequences of such an action.

Why does the non-native speaker take so long?

Many books have been written on language acquisition and much has been said about the difficulties of learning a second language.

"Some think that once this dominance of the intellectual over the emotional side occurs, we tend to overanalyze and not be 'free' enough in our efforts to learn a second language" (*Teaching Tactics for Japanese English Classrooms* by John Wharton).

Most people accept that the difficulty of learning a second language is greater for adults than for children. "Unlike children, it's possible that adult second language learners have become too rigid to just 'go with the flow' in order to learn as easily as their infantile counterparts" (*Teaching Tactics for Japanese English Classrooms* by John Wharton).

When talking about Asher's Total Physical Response, which means moving about the classroom, Wharton says Asher believes that movement reinforces the language lesson. Apparently, impressive results have been obtained with TPR. Asher's TPR is simply the giving of a name to an essential part of teaching. When we are young, we need to physically move our bodies in order to learn anything. The toddler uses his whole body, the child uses arms and legs, and an older child uses his fingers. No matter what age we reach, when a difficult problem appears, we reach for a pencil or a physical object to ease our understanding. An interesting aspect of this fact is seen daily in Japan. The Japanese language is so difficult that it is common to see an adult checking the spelling of a word by writing the word on the palm of his left hand with the index finger of his right hand. TPR works—there is no doubt about that—but some of us are given tiny little spaces in which to teach, and the ability to move even as much as an arm is extremely limited. It is also unnecessary when teaching adult classes. A well-prepared aim, well taught, will do all that is required.

We have already looked at some of the technical reasons as to why it takes an adult so long to learn a second language. There are also time constraints, teaching material problems, and staff problems. But these are the only reasons, and they are easily overcome. One of the main reasons that a non-native speaker takes so long to learn a language is because they normally have only one lesson per week. It takes a non-native speaker ten years to learn a second language, but a native speaker learns his own language in two years. Mathematically, it looks bad:

Table #24

Native speaker

two years = 104 (weeks) x 7 (days) x 10 (hours) (babies sleep long) = 7280 hours.

<u>Non-native speaker</u>

40 (weeks in school year) x 1 (hours of tuition) x 10 (years) = 400 hours

This does not compare well with the 7280 hours of the native speaker until one considers how much of a baby's waking time is spent in learning language. The non-native speaker can be fluent in English after ten years of lessons consisting of one hour per week, but much depends on the school, the head teacher, and the teacher in the classroom.

If only non-native English speaking teachers are used, then the students will not be able to fare well in the rhythm of the language and that is one of the major points of learning a language. Hence the need for the native English speaker. You, the native English speaker, the expert, have no time to mess around. Time is of the essence and much has to be covered in order to achieve fluency after ten years.

The other most important reason for non-native speakers taking so long to learn a language is that they subject themselves to poorer and poorer teachers. The baby, who learns a language in two years, has the best teacher: himself. Then he has the second-best teacher: his mother. Thereafter, the child improves, but the ability of the teachers diminishes. There are five ways into the brain: sight, sound, taste, smell and touch. Most teachers use only two of these ports—eyes and ears. A baby is not content to use only two. He uses all five. By introducing touch, a teacher is using three of the five senses, raising the teaching standard to three out of five. Every baby teaches himself at a rate of five out of five. Every baby touches, smells, tastes, looks at, and listens to everything.

It has been argued that adults take so long to learn a second language because an adult has so many more things to do and to study than a baby. This is simply not true. No one has more to do, or more to learn, than a baby. In two years the baby learns to walk, to talk, to manipulate his body, to use tools . . . The list is endless. Any adult achieving any one of these, in any given two years, is justifiably proud of himself.

Why does the baby learn so quickly?

The effort that a baby puts into learning language may not be apparent to everyone, but careful observation shows tremendous effort on the part of the baby. When a baby hears his mother's voice, he listens intently and tries hard to focus on her. Then he tries to do it himself. He tries to make the same sounds. He is now teaching himself pronunciation. The effort that the baby puts into learning to twist and shape

177

his mouth is amazing. Then, when he can make the sounds, he learns vocabulary.

> By 18 months, the infant language student is stringing words together in two and three-word "sentences"— usually called "telegraphic" utterances due to their simple and effective content. By age three he can chatter incessantly. . . . First language acquisition occurs at a rapid pace and without apparent effort by a process called "grammar construction" – basically just trial and error usage of words and phrases heard around them. (*Teaching Tactics for Japanese English Classrooms* by John Wharton)

By age three, a child certainly can chatter incessantly, but so can many two-year-olds. Either way, all agree that the baby learns very fast.

> The great linguist, Noam Chomsky, was among those who suggested that we have within us the innate capacity to learn language, by a "Language Acquisition Device" or LAD. This LAD allows us to distinguish speech sounds from other environmental noise and construct the simplest possible system of language out of the language around us. (*Teaching Tactics for Japanese English Classrooms* by John Wharton)

This may be true, but many babies refer to dogs as "bow-wows," and, in the age of steam locomotives, many referred to trains as "choo-choos." It may be that many more of a baby's unintelligible utterances are in fact sounds made by other things for which the baby has not yet learned the name.

> Behaviorists like B.F. Skinner believe that we learn by
> "operant conditioning," that is, the child "operates"
> language to get what it desires. And if "want milk"
> makes Mom produce the good stuff, the lesson is
> learned. (*Teaching Tactics for Japanese English Classrooms*
> by John Wharton)

Wharton says that this theory is unproven. It does, however, make sense. If, as I suggested earlier, the baby uses noises to signify items, he could well try "glug-glug" when he wants some milk. If this does not produce milk, then the baby will try something else. Babies always work very hard at language acquisition, and they are not always helped by anyone, not even by their own family. Many mothers have been known to teach their babies "bow-wow" for dog, "gang-gang-gang" for level crossing, and even "bishy-bishy-boo" for toilet. Some babies are, in fact, actually learning two languages at the same time.

As professional teachers, we do not have the freedom to do this. We must analyse what we do and what we teach.

Many years ago, as a lecturer in Education, I was advising on teaching techniques to young women training for the NNEB certificate, planning to go on to become nursery nurses. I gave them some teaching experiments to do because, as Confucius advised, I wanted them to do and thereby to understand. I explained to them that young children use all five senses when they learn and that they should try to use as many of the children's senses as possible. They were then asked to teach the children that gradients, weights, and textures of objects affect the speed at which the object will slide down a given slope. They split into groups, and each group had a different teaching method to investigate. Group

A were taught using eyes and ears only. They watched what was done and heard what was happening. Group B used three senses. They were taught as above but they were told to feel the surfaces. Group C were taught using hearing, sight, touch and smell. The boxes, which they had been given to slide down the slope, had been used to store different substances such as onion, plasticine, soap, air freshener, etc. Group D used all five senses. They were given boxes of condensed milk, face cream, milk, custard, etc. and asked to differentiate by sight or smell. They could not and so, with parental permission, they were given a globule of it to taste.

Two months later, Group A remembered doing the experiment but none of the results. Group B remembered the experiment but could provide only normal observances of speed and gradient. Group C remembered that the onion-smelling box was slowest no matter what gradient was used. Group D remembered everything clearly, and their interest in the experiment was still very much alive. Group A were totally uninterested in the subject.

Using the sense of taste is dangerous. Mothers, from a point of view of safety, remove any object that a baby puts into his mouth. This is natural. Safety far outweighs education. Teachers may not put objects into children's mouths nor encourage children to taste unknown substances. This makes teaching at a rate of five out of five all but impossible. This is acceptable, but teaching at a rate of two out of five is not. Teaching at a rate of two out of five is teaching at a failure rate. What can be done?

If mothers, when removing objects from a baby's mouth, talk to the baby about the feeling and the taste of the object while at the same time talking about the dangers inherent in putting objects into the mouth, much will be gained. It is irrelevant whether the baby understands or not. The object will have been removed, the mother will have given the baby more language input, and the baby will have gained more than if the object were silently removed.

Teachers can talk to their pupils about the taste of objects and about the smell of objects thereby bringing these senses to the fore prior to a lesson. Teachers should awaken all senses before trying to teach. "Awaken All Senses First" should be a teaching motto. In doing so, the teacher is increasing the chances of pupils remembering lessons.

Teachers must try to remember that children do not fail. They must always remember that children cannot fail. It is only teachers who fail. All babies learn to walk and talk within two years. This is because they have the world's best teacher. They teach themselves! It is the baby who is the best teacher of all, and it is he that we must look to when we need advice on teaching. As teachers, we must learn to listen to the children. We must try to learn from them!

That we may never forget it, let me repeat a previous passage:

D. C. Winnicot, child development expert, put forward the theory that "The Mother" was the best possible teacher that anyone could have. And certainly you must be impressed if you read his reasoned arguments and view the results of his research; if you watch any mother, even the newest recruit, slowly, gently, carefully and patiently guiding her baby, step-by-step to the completion of his studies. What impresses me most is that no mother has ever been heard to offer the excuses that have often been heard from professional teachers. "My student is not so bright," "I have no time to wait until he grasps the point," "He never takes clear notes," "He needs to go to a special school," "He does not listen to me." Every mother thinks that her baby, her pupil, is the cleverest pupil around. She is a dedicated teacher. Even extremely unintelligent mothers can have their babies speaking, walking, etc. within the two years. It is so easy to think that the mother is the best teacher of all, but in fact, it is the child himself who is teaching himself.

It is amusing to see parents trying to teach babies how to walk. So often, the mother will stand with the baby and direct him to the father who waits less than a metre in front of them. Both parents try to encourage the baby to walk forward. The cute little charmer, however, will have none of it. He knows that babies learn to walk sideways before they learn to walk forward. Walking sideways with an open-close shuffle eliminates the need to balance. Most babies will walk around a room sideways while holding onto the furniture before they will venture forward. Most parents know this, and yet they will still try to send the baby from the one parent to the other by asking him to walk forwards. Walking forwards with a small body and a large heavy head is all but impossible, and trying to encourage this will in fact hold the baby back rather than aid him. The baby learns to walk despite the efforts of the parents.

Babies may not know many facts, but they do know how to teach, and they do know how to learn. So do young children. So do young adults. It is the parents and the teachers who have forgotten. All babies love to learn. All young children love to learn. Even more amazing is the fact that babies and young children love to practice and love to do homework—not the stuff set by teachers but the things that they themselves know to be useful.

Try to teach a child to whistle, and you will soon regret having done so. Most children will drive everyone mad as they practice and practice this new skill. Yet some children do not! They give up immediately. They have already been taught failure, and they now know that they cannot learn this new skill. This is sad. The love of learning has already been killed. Who is it then that quenches this fire, this love of learning? There is only one answer to that. It is teachers who kill the love of learning. Sometimes it is a parent who took on the role of teacher and sometimes it is an older brother or sister. We as professional teachers must not kill that love.

In Scottish Academy, our motto is "To produce happy children who want to learn." Learning facts is not important. If as a teacher, you have taught a student many things but have made it a heavy, difficult task, you have not helped the student at all. If, as a teacher, you instill a love of learning into your students, you have equipped them for life.

To this end a poem was written for teachers at our nursery school to learn, and consigning it to memory was considered the most important point of their teaching. The poem exhorted teachers to make the child want to learn by making sure that the children enjoyed the lessons. Teachers were told to remember that, if the teachers and the pupils are not having fun the teacher was in fact not teaching. The fact that it was a poem made it easy and pleasurable to learn and was therefore a perfect example of what we need to do as teachers.

When training young teachers in other establishments, the first question I ask to critique a teacher is, "How many of the children enjoyed the lesson?" If the teacher cannot answer the question, she cannot know whether she has earned her salary or not, because she cannot know if any of the children learned anything. If the teacher thinks that none of the children enjoyed the lesson, she has just taken money for a lesson that she did not teach. This shocks young teachers, but they do see that it makes sense, and most of them then go on to see how they can make the children enjoy the lesson.

As teachers, we must always remember that children love to learn, so making sure that they enjoy a lesson is fairly simple. There is no need for theatrical displays or productions. Well-planned lessons with clearly defined aims that the children can see will ensure that they enjoy the lesson.

The younger the pupil, the harder it is to teach. A very young child cannot sit still for long and must always be moving. This must be part of the teaching plan. Move them at the beginning of the lesson, and they will happily sit still and learn the rest of the lesson. If the teaching is bad, the very young child will simply run away. Bad teaching in an adult class is not so horrendous. Adult students will sit and pretend to listen. They will look up the information later and try to learn things that were not taught. The adult student is there by choice, and the goal that brought them there in the first place will propel them along and make them learn. Young pupils are not there by choice. They are mostly there because adults, usually their mothers, sent them there. They have no goal but to reach the end of the lesson and to extract what pleasure they can during the lesson, usually by annoying the teacher.

When

English is taught as a foreign language all over the
world and has been for many, many years. In Japan it
is a fairly recent phenomenon. "The need for English grew
when Japan fully opened its doors to the outside world in
1868" (*English Language Education in Japan* – Hideo Oka –
July 2010). Technically, this may certainly be the case, but
prior to that, there was some to-ing and fro-ing. "In 1863
Thomas Glover helped the Chosu Five to study in Britain"
(*The Scottish Samurai* by Alexander MacKay).

[W]hen Japan emerged from two successful wars
against China (in 1892) and Russia (in 1904),
brimming with self-confidence. English was no longer
seen as an essential instrument for modernization;
instead, learning English was reduced to a kind
of cultural pursuit. The task of teaching English
shifted from foreign teachers to Japanese teachers,
consequently the teaching method became more
grammar-translation oriented. It was deemed a
landmark development when the famous writer
Soseki Natsume replace Lafcadio Hearn as English
lecturer at the university of Tokyo in 1903. . . . The
feverish rush into practical English reached a climax

185

at the time of the Tokyo Olympic Games in 1964 and again during the world exposition in Osaka in 1970. (*English Language Education in Japan* – Hideo Oka – July 2010)

All of these were a long time ago, and yet there is still much to be improved in the teaching of English to Japanese students. There is a school of thought that thinks that it is sufficient to give the students a base in English and thereafter allow them to perfect it themselves. Many students do this by going abroad to perfect their English in an English-speaking country. There are two huge problems in this way of thinking. The first is that, of course, there are not many students who have the opportunity to go abroad. The other problem is that native-speaking adults do not think it good manners to correct the mistakes of an adult foreigner, and some even find the mistakes quite cute. The higher the position of the foreign adult, the less likely it is that anyone will correct mistakes. On the other hand, everyone feels comfortable correcting a child's language mistakes, and native-speaking adults do so automatically.

One class of students that I taught in Japan had adult students who had lived and worked in Britain for many years, but they still had some quite bad mistakes. No one had ever told them about their mistakes, and they were quite horrified to find out that there were aspects of English that they had totally missed. Their basic English was fine, and their practical English was good, but they were still far from perfect.

This feverish rush into practical English that Oka tells us about happened in time for the Olympic Games in 1964— almost one hundred years after English was considered necessary. To cater to this trend, English as a second language was then taught in schools.

"In the year 2000 . . . . [t]he total number of hours of English instruction during eight years of formal schooling thus comes to well over 800 hours. . . . At the time of the Tokyo Olympic Games in 1964, there was a similar craze for practical English conversation among the general public" (*English Language Education in Japan* – Hideo Oka – July 2010). Despite this massive amount of English being taught to all Japanese schoolchildren in junior high schools, the results are not as impressive as they could or should be. Oka puts this down to the fact that the students had no confidence in their ability. He also thinks that despite the hours dedicated to the subject of English, it fails to achieve what could be expected because it is thought that "communicative competence is too distant a goal" (*English Language Education in Japan* – Hideo Oka – July 2010).

Despite the fact that time is dedicated to oral communication in Senior High School the standard of spoken English may be falling. "[H]igh school graduates will have no more than 2,700 words at their disposal. The decline is conspicuous because only a few decades ago high school students were expected to master no less than 3500 words" (*English Language Education in Japan* – Hideo Oka – July 2010).

Japan was aware of this situation, and Oka tells us that in order to improve it, the JET programme was introduced in 1987. This programme helped tremendously. Many native English speakers were brought to Japan to work in schools as Assistant Language Teachers. "As of 2001, there were 6190 foreign university graduates working as assistant teachers in languages classes in Japan" (*English Language Education in Japan* – Hideo Oka – July 2010).

Although this helped the situation greatly, the students were not speaking fluently and confidently. Oka pointed out that there were problems with the way of teaching, too, but that that would be put to rights. "To make this possible, the Ministry of Education launched a rigorous plan in 2003 to retrain all the 60,000 English teachers in public schools across the country" (*English Language Education in Japan* – Hideo Oka – July 2010).

Oka also stated that there were problems not only with the teachers but with the students themselves. He looked at the differences in attitudes of the students depending on whether they were junior high school students, senior high school students or university students. "[J]unior high schools students are still active in class and may even volunteer to answer. . . . [U]niversity students are just as listless as high school students are" (*English Language Education in Japan* – Hideo Oka – July 2010).

Oka then looked at the English teaching situation in primary schools. "It will be taught one hour a week as part of a 'foreign language activities' class, to be formally enforced in 2011 across the nation" (*English Language Education in Japan* – Hideo Oka – July 2010). Although this is an admirable state of affairs, there are many who think that it is impossible to become fluent with only one lesson per week, and so parents seek more English education for their children. It is perfectly possible for students to become fluent in English conversation with only one lesson per week if a strict teaching discipline is adhered to by both the school and the teachers.

When teaching EFL teachers to teach English, I always tell them to plan for ten years of forty lessons per year. In this plan, they naturally must cover all the eight points of learning English (Listening, Pronunciation, Vocabulary,

Rhythm, Speaking, Reading, Writing, and Grammar), and they must ensure that every student covers all of these points and that they progress from Listening at the beginning to Grammar at the end. It is not, however, as straightforward as it appears. Learning has often been referred to as a curve, but in fact, it is probably more correct to liken it to ascending a spiral staircase. Using this as a guide, it follows then that the students must always be taught Listening lessons even in their final year, and that they must also be taught Grammar in their first year. The following chart compiled by one of my students shows the plan perfectly.

	1st year	2nd year	3rd year	4th year	5th year	6th year	7th year	8th year	9th year	10th year
1	L	L	L	L	L	L	L	L	L	L
2	L	L	L	L	L	L	L	L	L	P
3	L	L	L	L	L	L	L	L	P	V
4	L	L	L	L	L	P	P	P	V	Rh
5	L	L	L	L	P	P	P	P	V	Rh
6	L	L	L	L	P	P	P	V	V	Rh
7	L	L	L	L	P	P	P	V	Rh	Rh
8	L	L	L	P	P	P	V	V	Rh	S
9	L	P	P	P	P	V	V	Rh	Rh	S
10	P	P	P	P	P	V	Rh	Rh	Rh	S
11	P	P	P	P	V	V	Rh	Rh	S	S
12	P	P	P	P	V	Rh	Rh	Rh	S	R
13	P	P	P	V	V	Rh	Rh	S	S	R
14	P	P	V	V	V	Rh	S	S	S	R
15	P	P	V	V	V	Rh	S	S	S	R
16	P	V	V	V	Rh	Rh	S	S	R	R
17	P	V	V	V	Rh	Rh	S	R	R	R
18	P	V	V	V	Rh	S	S	R	R	R
19	P	V	V	Rh	Rh	S	R	R	R	R
20	V	V	V	Rh	Rh	S	R	R	R	W
21	V	V	V	Rh	Rh	S	R	R	R	W
22	V	V	Rh	Rh	S	S	R	R	R	W
23	V	V	Rh	Rh	Rh	S	R	R	W	W
24	V	V	Rh	Rh	S	R	R	W	W	W
25	V	Rh	Rh	S	S	R	W	W	W	W
26	V	Rh	Rh	S	S	R	W	W	W	W
27	V	Rh	S	S	S	R	W	W	W	W
28	Rh	Rh	S	S	R	W	W	W	W	W
29	Rh	Rh	S	S	R	W	W	W	W	G
30	Rh	S	S	S	R	W	W	W	W	G
31	Rh	S	S	R	R	W	G	G	G	G
32	Rh	S	S	R	R	W	G	G	G	G
33	S	S	R	R	W	W	G	G	G	G
34	S	S	R	R	W	G	G	G	G	G
35	S	S	R	W	W	G	G	G	G	G
36	S	R	R	W	W	G	G	G	G	G
37	S	R	W	W	W	G	G	G	G	G
38	R	W	W	G	G	G	G	G	G	G
39	W	W	G	G	G	G	G	G	G	G

A quick glance at the chart is sufficient to see that not all of the eight subjects are covered every year. In the first year, there is only one lesson on writing and none on grammar. In the second year, there are two lessons on writing and none on grammar. Similarly, in the last year, there is only one lesson on listening, but at least there is one. The chart is, therefore, not ideal as each year the students should cover all subjects. Nonetheless, this is an excellent example of a ten-year plan. It is also a perfectly suited to Murayama-San, as she was not comfortable teaching grammar to first-year students. This is as it should be. If she is not comfortable doing it, then it would not be a good lesson. Murayama-San went further and colour-coded each section so that it could be seen at a glance when each subject changed.

In year one, the emphasis is on Pronunciation but teaching the lessons in English means that although the aim of the lesson is Pronunciation, the children are having to listen to the lesson and so Listening is also involved. The teacher will automatically be using an English rhythm and grammar will be covered automatically too, as the teacher changes verb endings to suit different subjects and tenses. By teaching in English, new vocabulary will be introduced automatically, and so there only remains Reading and Spelling to cover in order to have all eight subjects covered in every lesson. The children will be covering Speaking every time they answer, even if it is just to shout "Here!" when the roll is called.

How

Now comes perhaps the most important chapter of all: how to teach English. You can speak English, but can you teach it?

> Suppose we decided that we had to "teach" children to speak. How would we go about it? . . . Jerome Bruner has said that one thing that happens in school is that children are led to believe they don't know or can't do something that they knew, or could do, before they got to school. (*How Children Learn* by John Holt)

This may or may not be the case. One thing is certain is that most five-year-olds who go to school go there happily; year by year, resentment builds, until by the tenth year in school more than one quarter of these children who started school so happily and were so proud to go there hate it and are anxious to leave. We must work to change this.

Teacher trainers and child behaviourists use the acronym HATE to list the attributes that make up a child's personality. They are Heredity, Attitude, Training, and Environment. A closer look at these four areas will help greatly when considering how to teach. By the time the child has been born the effects, of Heredity have already taken place. In many ways, the Attitudes of the parents, too, are set (given that the child will continue to have the same set of parents until he reaches adulthood). The attitude of the parents greatly affects the child's future. The very intelligent son of a person who left school early, having hated it, is unlikely to go to university. "Secondly and much more important, the parents of almost all these children do not expect in the slightest that their children will later go on to a university" (*How Children Learn* by John Holt). However, the son of a lawyer or a doctor is likely to go to university regardless of how well he performs on intelligence tests.

Two of the four factors affecting personality remain: Environment and Training. Environment changes often and will change greatly if the parents move from country to country. Training is the realm of the teacher. As school teachers, we use the acronym PIES. These are the four areas of training needed: Physical training, Intellectual training, Emotional training and Social training. This, then, is the remit of the schools.

Each year schools, become bigger and better—at least, they tend to become bigger, but whether that is better is suspect. "[W]e have to have giant school-factories because we can't get good education in a school unless it has all the latest equipment" (*How Children Learn* by John Holt). As teachers, we must remember that a bad workman blames his tools. Excellent teaching can be done, and is done, in small village schools. No matter the work conditions, a good teacher teaches well and her students learn well.

In order to help student teachers teach to the best of their abilities, I conjured up the acronym OPERATE. Each letter stands for what must be done to achieve success. Teachers, in order to operate well, must Observe, Prepare, Evaluate, Review, Aim, Teach, and Evaluate once again. If you keep this word in mind, it will help you teach, and it will help you to teach well.

O is for Observation

A first lesson with any class is difficult. The first lesson is really just to meet students. In this first meeting, a lesson must be taught, but it should be a general let's-have-fun-in-English type of lesson, because the first lesson with a class is only for observation. The object of the first lesson should simply be to see what needs to be taught, to see what the students expect, to see the classroom, and to see how you yourself react to the class atmosphere. Until you understand the students in your class, you cannot teach well.

As a young teacher, I regularly had to teach fifty-two children in a class. Now I am called upon to teach eighty or ninety in a class. With good observation, this is no problem.

Observe everything and note it. The truth in this as a theory is very obvious even to the newly fledged teacher. So, also, is the impracticality of it. Nonetheless, in order to teach well, it must be done.

Teaching twenty to thirty fifteen-year-olds leaves little time for note taking. Since there are so many notes to be taken and as it is easier to score out than to write in, the compilation of charts listing the possibilities makes a great deal of sense. Compiling charts will not only simplify the taking of notes, it will also help to pinpoint what is meant by "everything" and why everything must be observed. Basically there are only three things making up "everything": the classroom, the students, and the teacher.

The Classroom

Some tools are excellent and some are pretty useless, but only a bad workman blames his tools. The classroom is a teaching tool. Make the best of what you have.

Working with blind, deaf, mentally handicapped, and physically handicapped children in the course of my studies allowed me to see many strange but effective classroom designs. In the school for the deaf, the teachers had to sit on the floor while the students sat on chairs. The theory behind this is that it is easier on the neck to look down for long periods of time rather than to keep looking up. When studying educational technology, one of my projects was to design a school. Unfortunately, most classrooms have not been designed by teachers. Most classrooms in which I had to teach left a lot to be desired. You will undoubtedly have to do a lot to your classroom to make it work for you. Making a chart of the classroom and keeping it handy will help.

Windows

Carefully mark where the windows are. The golden rule of teaching is never to stand with the windows behind you. Students are not known for their desire to look at the teacher all the time as it is, and if they have to screw up their eyes against the light to do so, they will be less likely to look at you.

Having the light behind you deprives you of your best weapon. Students will be unable to note your facial expressions. A tilt of the head with a simultaneous lift of the eyebrows can head off trouble at the pass, but for this to be effective, it must be seen clearly. Always make sure that the light falls upon your face not the back of your head. If necessary, move the desks around to accommodate the light.

Blackboard/Whiteboard

Do not stand between the students and the whiteboard and expect them to take note of what you have written there. They are more likely to take note of whether you are thinning on top, spreading at the hips, or wearing a peculiarly designed cardigan. These thoughts will certainly interest them more than anything that you have written for them. Make sure that there is somewhere to the left and to the right of the board where you can safely go when you wish to talk about anything that you have written. From this vantage point, you should be able to see all of the students, and they should not be able to see you if they are looking at the board. If this is the case, then you are in a perfect position to spot the first student who looks elsewhere before he or she has had a chance to catch the eye of another student. Allow this to happen, and your difficulties will rapidly pile up.

Clock

If it is difficult to see the clock without raising your head, bring your own clock and place it in such a position that your glance will be able to fall on it often and naturally during the course of the lesson. Students who see the teacher watching the clock will be made aware of the length of time the lesson is taking. They will also experience a feeling of rejection.

Pencil Sharpeners and Waste Bins

Position the pencil sharpener and the bin so that when you use them you do not have to turn your back on the class, and have them in a position so that when the children use them, they will be within your line of vision. The student at the pencil sharpener or at the bin often acts the clown for the benefit of the rest of the class. To guard against this trick, keep the bin and pencil sharpener in place where you can see anyone who is using them while you are watching the rest of the class.

Teacher's Chair

Make sure that the teacher is not occupying a space too high for student comfort. Stiff, craned necks do not make for good attention. A good way to ensure against this is to move around the classroom, allowing the students to move their necks into different positions. This is especially important for tall teachers. Another good point is that moving around helps to keep the troublemakers in view.

The Students

On the first day in a new class, while taking the attendance, write the children's names onto the plan that you have made of the classroom. Write their names onto appropriate squares, signifying the desks which they are occupying. This will help your observation skills. Later, you may not recall a student's name but you will quite possibly recall where he sat.

Even on the first day, the potential troublemakers should be obvious. They are probably sitting at the back of the class and/or lounging in their seats. When a lounger is spotted, the teacher should immediately start to move the students around on the pretext of helping the student to see or to hear better. When moving the lounger to another seat, tell him that you are presuming that he was forced to take up that awkward position due to an inability to hear. This will let the students know immediately that you are a teacher who will take immediate action if they misbehave and that you can spot a troublemaker a mile away. They will then respect you for having sussed out the potential troublemaker. It will also allow you to act with kindness instead of with anger. Many students feel that they have succeeded in school that day if they have made the teacher angry. Do not accommodate them.

Favouritism/Discrimination

Mark on your sheet the desks at which you stood during a lesson. Over a period of time it will become obvious if you are tending to go to one desk in particular, and it will also help to pinpoint any desks to which you do not gravitate.

Children's Desks

Crossing off the empty desks on a chart will help you to become aware not only of absences, but also of children who never seem to sit in their seats for long. These children are not troublemakers, but their nomadic class style helps them to evade the teacher and her teaching.

The Students' Appearance and Mannerisms

Mark the following: what the students wear and what their hairstyles are; what you wore; who smiled and who scowled. This cannot be done in one lesson, but a goodly amount of observation of this kind should be recorded at each and every lesson, even after the class has finished. You will be surprised how quickly you become able to record this kind of information until one day you will find yourself able to record as you teach.

I recommend a personal shorthand for this. The base of my personal shorthand is that on my plan of the classroom, instead of squares to represent desks, I plot out the classroom on my first day using circles. These represent the students. It is then an easy matter to draw in long hair, a smile or a scowl. If the student is neatly and tidily dressed I put a tick beside the circle. These circles can be filled in while marking the attendance on the first day. If a space is left below each circle the name of the student can be written underneath as the attendance is taken and the appropriate symbols filled in at the same time.

The Teacher

The aim of this book is to help you teach, but more importantly, it is to help you teach your students YOUR WAY. You are the teacher. No one else knows your class quite as well as you do. No one can possibly understand the type of chemistry that goes on between you and your class. Human relationships, be they peer to peer, man to woman, mother to child, or teacher to class, differ each and every time. No one interacts with your class in the same way that you do. Therefore, no one can tell you how to teach.

This relationship between yourself and your class is the very base of your teaching. Use it to keep your students interested and happy. A student who enjoys his lesson but learns nothing will come again for a second lesson, and the teacher manages to have two bites at the cherry. The student who has learned much but was worked too hard or was bored will cease the lessons as soon as possible. This is one reason why charts work. You can mark in which children enjoyed the lesson and which did not. There is no need to record more than two students: the one who did and the one who did not.

If there is much personal information about the students to be recorded on charts, it is better that it is done at home and not brought into school. Students will resent this information being seen by others. Keep a book or a file at home. Fill in a paper in the classroom each time and then take it home to add to the information there.

These observations may seem to be an incredible amount of work, and they are, but they help tremendously. The effect on the entire class is wonderful when you throw out an observation such as that the student has had a haircut or has donned a new colour of clothing. If your students are babies, they should be praised and admired when mentioning your observations.

A good phrase to keep in mind is: the older the student, the less the praise! For older students, quips are better. "I see you've had a haircut. Well, now that your brain can breathe better, can we expect better work?" This kind of quip is very acceptable. The student will know that you have observed him, and he will feel proud. The class will laugh, and he will be a hero for a few seconds. "I see you've had a haircut. It's beautiful." This is unacceptable. The student will hate you. The rest of the class will laugh, but they will torment him afterwards. "I see you've had a haircut. Did they find any brains?" This, too, is unacceptable. The students will laugh. The student himself may well laugh, but it belittles the teacher to stoop so low. There will also be one student in the class who would hate to be the butt of such a statement, and that student will instantly resent such a teacher. If you are not good at finding witty, non-sarcastic quips, simply stick to a sudden pointing of the finger in the student's direction— at the most unexpected time is best—and saying, "Haircut!" This will achieve results that are almost as good. The student will feel honoured at being noticed and singled out; the class will laugh at and appreciate the sudden interruption. Marking your observations in your book will also help you to guard against favouritism. Always mark which students have earned one of your comments.

A final and, of course, very important piece of observation is which students need what help. This is done by marking three children into the chart with the letters VG, G or NG. This will let you see who did exceptionally well, who was good, and who was no good . This kind of marking will not only help you to teach better by knowing who needs what help, but it will also help you to write your end-of-term report in minutes instead of hours.

P is for Preparation

Lesson preparation is an essential part of teaching, but it is not the whole of teaching. The maximum amount of time to be spent preparing a one-hour lesson should be ten minutes. Teaching is not done at home or in a staffroom. It is done in the classroom in front of the students. Preparation done at home should be as outlined in Observation.

Over-preparation is far worse than under-preparation. Every teacher can wing a lesson or two. Wing too many and you will fall flat on your face, but with a good book outlining the aim and the steps to take to teach the lesson, under-preparation should not be lethal. Over-preparation can be fatal. One of the greatest dangers in over-preparing a lesson is that the teacher becomes unable to jettison it when it is going badly. This is unforgivable. "And whatever the game is, we must be ready to give it up, instantly and without regret, if the child is not enjoying it" (*How Children Learn* by John

Holt). If the students hate the lesson, they will not learn anything.

Every teacher has gone into a classroom to teach what she thinks will be an admirable lesson only to find that the students already know it, and so it is too easy for them, so they are bored; that it is too difficult for them, so they are bored; or that it is not interesting enough for them, so they are bored. For any of these reasons, a lesson must be instantly abandoned. The students should not suffer because of teacher incompetence. When a planned lesson does not go well, simply admit defeat and proceed to give the students a game. Any game in English will turn up some previously unknown fact, giving food for a future lesson, and at the same time, it will continue to stimulate your class.

A lesson forced down the throats of the students who gave you the courtesy of attending your class will not be able to be digested. The students may sit there and take it, but you will have put a great nail in your own coffin. Many students in the class will hold it against you. One or two uninteresting lessons they can forgive, but too many and they will become sullen and withdrawn if not downright rebellious. Students have the right to have interesting lessons.

Although little preparation is needed for the lessons, a great amount of preparation must be done on the teacher. Self-preparation cannot be stressed enough. Make sure that you have sufficient sleep the night before. Students do not deserve tired, jaded teachers. Before retiring for the night, look over your clothes for the morning. It goes without saying that they must be neat and clean but they must also be well chosen. Naturally, the students will be critical, and they will scrutinize everything that you wear. The result should be admiration. That, however, is but a small part of the problem.

The teacher's clothes should not draw attention away from her face. I have, on several occasions, had to point out to a teacher that she stabbed herself in the back by wearing a pair of gorgeous, sparkly shoes. During her lesson, she had to repeatedly tell the students to pay attention. In fact, the students were paying attention—they were paying a great deal of attention, not to her lesson, but to her shoes. They were trying very hard to bring the shoes to the attention of the students at the back of the room, who then became engrossed in trying to find a way to see the shoes.

Teachers' clothes should be dark and non-descript, with a bright collar or some interesting novelty up at the neck, on the hair, or on the head. That will keep the attention of the students riveted where you want it. Male teachers should, however, guard against flamboyant ties. Being long and narrow, ties tend to pull the attention down from the face, and students then start to assess the abdominal muscles of the male teacher, or the lack of them. Do not aid them in this scrutiny. Female teachers have an easier task, as they can simply apply bright lipstick prior to teaching, and that will help to solicit attention to the face. Male teachers normally have it easier when it comes to footwear. It is easy for them to wear non-descript shoes and socks. This is more difficult for female teachers. A female teacher should, however, try not to wear bright shoes or socks, or in any other way divert attention away from her own face.

Spend some of your preparation time on your hands. A teacher's hands are often on display, and the students are unforgiving of bitten nails, chipped nails, or grimy, dirty-looking hands. However the opposite is just as bad. No bright red, heavily painted nails, please. No heavy, overpowering rings. Keep the hands simple and unremarkable. In this way, it will be easier to hold the attention of your class.

Some preparation time must also be spent on transportation. Check how you are going to arrive at your class. Check timetables if you need to use public transport. Check the weather, too. You must not arrive late, overheated, or bedraggled. The students must know that you care.

E is for Evaluate

After your preparation, always go over it again. It is amazing how often teachers prepare work and then leave it alone. It must be evaluated.

First, you must ask yourself if the lesson is worthwhile. I once watched a young teacher teach a passable lesson but when I asked her if she had evaluated her lesson she seemed puzzled. She had begun her lesson by entering the class and saying, "Hello." Naturally, the children thought that that is what should be said. When I asked her if she had any problem with the children saying "Hello," she said that she had no problem at all. When I asked her how she thought I would feel if I entered a classroom and the students said, "Hello," to me, she blushed. She had not thought about it from anyone's point of view except her own. She had not evaluated her lesson.

Evaluate the books that you or your students will use. Many books that purport to teach English carry incredibly bad examples of English that should never be spoken. You are the native speaker. You are the expert. Run everything through the mother/teacher/bar scenarios and then ask yourself if the English in the book is acceptable English for your students to use. If not, explain when it could be used but that some other phrase is better. In this way you can still follow the book while giving the students acceptable English. If, after running an English phrase or sentence through the mother/teacher/bar scenarios, you are still unsure then make yourself adopt the correct posture when saying some of these English stereotypes. One of the common English sentences in books that should never be taught is the, "My name is . . . " one. This sentence goes well with a hands-on-the-hips attitude and head thrown back. This should be enough to tell you that it is not acceptable.

Evaluate your clothes. When you turn to write on the board, the children will have a field day. Is your blouse too tight? Does your shirt show a roll of fat at the top of your trousers? Take these things into consideration. Will you have to bend down during your lesson? Will your clothes allow for that? Will you have to walk quickly up the aisle between the desks to head off any trouble? Will your shoes herald your arrival from way off, or will they allow you to move quietly and swiftly to the area of the disturbance? Will your hair stay in place during the lesson?

R is for Review

When all is ready and has been evaluated, review everything that you have done. It need not take long. Two or three minutes should suffice, but you must review your observation chart, your aim, your plan, and your clothes.

Teaching can be a nerve-wracking procedure at times, and many teachers, male and female, give away their nervousness to the students by gestures such as the continual flicking of a lock of hair that will not stay in place. This will invite trouble.

Many young male teachers are guilty of this, and then they are surprised when the rogues of the class start to play up. Never underestimate the students. They have spent years judging teachers by their clothes and their gestures. I have seen a teacher brought to grief by continually tucking a stray wisp of hair behind her ear and another by the continual pushing of a pair of glasses back up onto the bridge of his nose.

If your glasses tend to slide down your face, tighten them before you go to your lesson. If a lock of hair needs to stay tucked behind your ears, spray it with a stiff hair lacquer. If you have a lock of hair that flops down over your face, you may be better to consider cutting it rather than giving your students an action to parody or an occasion to giggle each time you flick the lock. You may not know that you are doing it but the students will.

A is for Aim

It is impossible to teach a lesson without an aim. Teaching a lesson without an aim is akin to playing football without a goal. It could be called a kick-about, but not football. Similarly, a teacher in a classroom without an aim could be said to be kicking-about but not teaching.

Decide on an aim. Make it simple. Take the Americans' advise and KISS it (Keep It Simple, Stupid). Recently I have heard it referred to as Keep It Simple, Sweetie. Either way, the message is clear, and it is excellent advice.

Many years ago, while critiquing a young student teacher in a lesson I explained that she failed to teach the lesson because she had not made a clear and simple aim. She was quite astonished and told me that she had had an aim, but that she found it difficult to achieve. When I asked her what her aim was, I found out that it was to teach that the –ing format follows the word *is*. The aim was fine. When I asked her for whom this aim was intended, she told me it was for the class. I was shocked. I told her that no one can teach a lesson to more than one student at one time. Now she was shocked. Using the football analogy, I showed her that she was attempting to score twenty-two goals with one ball or one goal while kicking twenty-two balls at the same time. Either way will result in a decided failure to score.

Choose one student for the aim that is intended and make absolutely sure that that one student is interested and that this one student has learned the aim at the end of the lesson beyond the slightest shadow of a doubt. In this way, you can be absolutely sure that one student knows the formula. Many of the other children will have picked up the point, too. Because the lesson was aimed at one particular student, it will have appeal to that particular type of boy, and so it will appeal to all boys of that type. The clever and the studious children will learn it anyway, and so the amount of children learning the lesson is greatly increased. While teaching the lesson, you can observe who did not understand or catch the lesson. This can be noted and worked on later. Assuming that you have forty lessons a year and that you have forty students or fewer in the class, this method will ensure that each student has a hand tailored lesson perfectly geared to his temperament and ability. Nothing could be better.

T is for Teach

Enjoy your teaching. If you are not looking forward to the lesson, what chance have the students?

If you spend time in the staffroom prior to your lesson, make sure that you leave it in time. Never let it be thought by the students that you do not want to go to your lesson. If the teacher does not approach the lesson with joy and anticipation, neither will the students.

For this reason, always make sure that you eat a hearty breakfast. However, if your lesson is after lunch, do not eat too much. On a number of occasions, I have sent a teacher home who had obviously had no breakfast and who ran out of energy before the end of the lesson. If you simply cannot face breakfast in the morning, make sure that you have a sugary drink or a hard sweetie to give your system a boost. Teaching is tiring work. The students deserve an animated lesson.

Much has been said about motivation in teaching, but it is not needed. Interesting lessons well taught will suffice to capture the interest of students. Babies love to learn; so do young children. Even adults!

> It is hard not to feel that there must be something very wrong with much of what we do in school, if we feel the need to worry so much about what many people call "motivation." . . . [Children's] curiosity grows by what it feeds on. Our task is to keep it well supplied with food . . . like taking them to a supermarket with no junk food in it. (*How Children Learn* by John Holt)

E is for Evaluate

Once again, evaluation is needed. But this time you must evaluate your lesson. When the lesson is finished, even if you are hurrying on to the next lesson, take a minute to mark in any student who did not appear to understand, any who misbehaved in any way (they did not like that type of lesson), and any who smiled and gave you their attention. For the latter group, the lesson succeeded. You must also mark which students had difficulty with any part of your lesson, but most importantly of all, you must mark where you stood when you were teaching. Many teachers fail because they tend to keep to one part of the classroom, thereby aiding and abetting the students who want to hide and create mischief. It also shows favouritism, albeit unintended, to the students near where the teacher stands.

Ideally, the marks on the paper showing where you stood, at any time, should be dotted all over the plan of the classroom but, as no one has ever taught an ideal lesson, it will probably be very lopsided. This if fine provided that you take heed of it and make sure that you stand in some other places the next time. Over a period of a month, four lessons, the entire classroom should be covered. To ensure this, it is good to think of the classroom as having four areas; each one must be covered each week. Some student teachers have chosen north, south, east, and west areas. This will work provided that one of these areas is not all windows. Stay away from the windows! The students cannot be expected to look into the light to see the teacher. If one of your walls is entirely a bank of windows, then try to choose corners so that at least you have a margin of safety.

Evaluate your own teaching. Make sure that you challenge your students, not threaten them.

A challenge is something that will stretch your powers with the likelihood of confirming them; you want to take on a challenge because you have confidence enough that you can succeed. A threat is a task that seems beyond your powers to accomplish or cope with. (*How Children Learn* by John Holt)

Students will often feel threatened if they fail to understand, or worse still if they misunderstand. Many times, teachers just seem to miss the fact that a student is on another wavelength. Think of yourself as a farmer sowing seed. If the ground is hard and brittle, the seed has no chance. In the case of rice, the farmer wants a field with two to three inches of water lying on top of the soil. For him, this is ideal. The farmer who is sowing barley will want a well-drained field. Neither is wrong. I have seen some well-planned lessons go awry because the student teacher failed to ensure that the students were on the correct wavelength.

A particularly good example of this happened with my own mother. My mother was eighty years old, and one of my sisters thought that she was beginning to show signs of Alzheimer's disease and wanted to have my mother tested. My mother lived in an old folk's home at that time, and my sister arranged for a psychiatrist to interview her. When my mother was told that she had a visitor and that he was waiting for her in the lounge she went along happily.

The man told her his name and there was a silence. He asked my mother if she was not going to give him her name.

She replied rather tersely, "You know my name."

The psychiatrist nodded sadly and informed her that this was the first time that they had met.

"I know that," she said, "but it is written on the paper in front of you."

Ignoring the bad start, the psychiatrist picked up the paper and wrote on it. Then he asked her if she knew the date.

"Don't you know the date?" she asked him.

"Yes," he said. "I know the date. I just wanted to know if you knew the date."

"I know the date," she answered.

"Could you tell me the date then?" he asked gently.

"You said you knew the date," she replied rather crossly.

The interview went downhill from there on. The most amazing part of it all was that after the psychiatrist had left, my mother went to the office and reported to staff there that she thought that they should call the police because a strange man had just been in the building asking strange questions. "I think he's not right in the head," she told them sadly.

A true story, a funny story, but it serves to show that one needs to be on the same wavelength. It happens often in normal everyday speech that one person is talking about a completely different thing than the other, but it eventually sorts itself out and no harm is done. Asking a few questions soon sorts out the miscommunication, and much humour is often extracted once the two people realise what has happened. This is not the case in teaching. Asking questions is bad teaching. Many educationalists have pointed this out time and time again, and yet it is a ploy still being used by many teachers.

> [T]oo much quizzing is likely to make him begin to think that learning does not mean figuring out how things work, but in getting and giving answers that please grown ups. . . . His reason for not answering the question "What's that?" may be only that the question itself confuses him, that he doesn't know what we want him to say or do. (*How Children Learn* by John Holt)

Once when I was a young teacher, a mother came to my classroom and told me that her seven-year old son had asked where he came from, and so she had given him a full biological explanation. I nodded my acknowledgement. "He said that he wanted to know it to tell the teacher. I thought that you had been teaching something in science, so I thought it best not to confuse him," she added.

"No," I replied, rather puzzled. "The subject has not been mentioned at all."

That evening, she asked her son why he wanted to know where babies came from. "Not babies. I wanted to know where I came from because there's a new boy in our class who came from London."

If members within a family or even adults in a strange situation can misinterpret a question, it stands to reason that students are much more likely to do so. "Dumb questions not only insult and anger children but often confuse them enough to destroy what they have already learned" (*How Children Learn* by John Holt). "[T]he anxiety children feel at constantly being tested, their fear of failure, punishment, and disgrace, severely reduces their ability both to perceive and remember" (*How Children Fail* by John Holt). "Because of these wrong judgments we label many, perhaps millions, of these children as having some kind of supposedly incurable 'learning disability'" (*How Children Learn* by John Holt).

Teachers should not ask questions, but children should. When they do, it is always wise to listen carefully to them when they ask questions or express doubt. The results may be funny, but much harm can be done by a teacher talking about one thing while a student is off on another tangent. If teaching sport, it can be downright dangerous. I teach skiing to our young nursery school students, and I impress upon the other teachers how important it is to tell the students exactly what it is that you want them to do. Make sure that they are given clear aims. Imagine my shock and horror, then, when my own advice backfired on me.

I had walked the students up the side of a gentle slope and set them up in the correct body position for skiing. In this pose, I sent them down the slope. The children improved tremendously and quickly. Empowered by the success of this, I quickly moved on to key phrases which, when said, allowed the children to take up the correct pose by themselves. "Skis together"—they placed their skis together with the valley ski slightly forward of the other. "Bend your knees"—they bent their knees and knelt down on the fronts of their boots pushing their shins into the top of the boots. "Zip to the sky"—they tucked in their rear ends and pointed their trouser zips upwards. Perfect! Off they went, and their positions were exemplary.

One of the five-year-olds, Coco Kanaya, had been skiing with us twice before, and she was wonderful. I decided to take her up another level. At the top of the slope, I told her how good she was and that I would try to take her up another level. She nodded wisely; she had seen the adults skiing and had watched them carefully. She knew what to do and she wanted desperately to ski as well as we could. I explained to her that she had been skiing on two skis, but in actual fact, we only ski on one foot, and indeed only on the big toe of that foot. She looked at me as though I was lying to her. "It's true," I said. "Ask the other teacher." She turned round and looked questioningly to the other teacher who simply nodded affirming that it was indeed the truth.

With that affirmation, Coco looked at us both as if we were really stupid, but in her estimation little more can be expected of teachers. She then pushed forward, ready to set off, and just before she did so, she took one foot and placed it on top of the other foot so that the two skis were actually at right angles to each other. Everyone burst out laughing. Everyone except Coco. She was so angry at the resulting laughter, and quite rightly so. Although everyone was laughing at Coco, they should have laughing at the incompetent teacher who told her to do that. I knew that for a fact, and I cringed.

I use this story to teach student teachers, and then I divide them into pairs with one ballpoint pen per pair. I use the type of pen that has a push button rather than a cap, as the push button pen contains a spring. The test is to take the pen apart. Then, one student tells the other what to do in order to reassemble the pen, and the other student, in true Coco fashion, is doing exactly, EXACTLY as he was told. This is always a hilarious lesson.

Teacher A: Lift the pen case.

Teacher B lifts the pen case using all her fingers in a fist and grabs the pen.

Teacher A: Hold the pen in two fingers.

Teacher B holds the pen as if it were a cigarette.

Teacher A continues to redirect teacher B until the pen is reassembled while Teacher B does exactly what she is told. Many teachers failed to reassemble the pen.

Naturally, in class, most students will understand what the teacher meant even if it is not actually what she said, and normally this is no problem. Someday, it will be. If it is not a mischievous child doing exactly as the pen assembler did, it may well be a child who has genuinely gone off at a tangent. Well-aimed lessons geared toward one child per lesson will guard against this.

One of my student teachers, James Leonard, commented that he had learned a lot about teaching EFL students, but he knew that eventually he would forget some or all of it. "What to do, then?" he asked. "If I am still in Japan, I can ask for advice, but what should I do if I am in another country? Who can I go to for advice?"

"Go to the baby. Every country has one-year-old babies who are learning their own language. Watch them carefully. In this way, you will always have a wonderful mentor close at hand."

Watch a baby closely learning his own language, then go back and do your homework. Analyse what you saw and how you can incorporate this into your lessons. Teachers should always do homework. They should never give it to the children. No teacher should ever need to set homework. If a lesson is well taught and the students have enjoyed it, the lesson will be remembered fondly and the student will be keen to forge ahead by himself.

When I was young, my mother told me that when I was fifteen years old and left school she would help me to find a good job. I was not happy. I wanted to stay on at school; I wanted to play more. I loved school. I did not want to have to work. On the pretext that it would secure me a better job, I begged to be allowed to continue at school for a few more years.

My father agreed. He told me that I would be allowed to stay on at school until I was eighteen on the premise that I brought no books into the house. He maintained that his home was for the family and that no one should be asked to accommodate anyone who selfishly wanted to do studying or homework, both of which he decided belonged solely in the realm of the school.

Each year, he wrote a letter to the headmaster of the school, telling him that I was not allowed to do homework or study at home. He maintained that the government of the country decreed that school was from 9:00 a.m. to 4:00 p.m., and that any teacher who could not teach sufficiently well during that time to allow the pupils to pass the tests should hand over part of her salary to him, and he would use the money to find a way around the problem.

When I left school and decided to go to college, I asked my father if he would remove the ban, but he refused. Each year he wrote a letter to the college explaining his principles. Despite this, or because of it, I passed all of my examinations and became a schoolteacher. By imposing homework and study bans, he made me dislike teachers who could not teach well and love those who could. If we had a poor teacher, the other pupils or students were able to go home and revise the lesson or learn it by themselves. I could not. Bad teaching infuriated me.

There is no need for teachers to set homework! Teach a child to whistle and watch him—or rather, listen to him—practice and practice and practice until he can finally whistle. Ask a child once to wink and then stand back and be entertained for a week or more as he practices how to wink. Encourage children, applaud their efforts, and the results are amazing. Children are harder taskmasters on themselves than any adult could be.

When I play English-speaking games with my students I am always amazed at how children force themselves to learn the part so that they may win. It is not uncommon to see the children cover their ears with their hands, close their eyes, and rock backward and forwards as they strive to learn the line that they must say in order to win a game.

Contrary to what most people think, the attention span of children is much more than that of adults. In search of more information on how to teach, I returned to college several times. As a mature student among other mature students, we often marvelled at how often, even during lessons of intense interest to us, our brain would suddenly go off at a tangent. Most of us agreed that questions such as, "Did I turn off the gas?" and "Do I need potatoes for tonight's dinner?" would suddenly simply pop into our heads with no indication that our thoughts had wandered. Children seldom do this.

> [A young child] tried to turn [the on-off switch] herself, but her fingers weren't strong enough. When this happened, she reached down, took my right hand, brought it up to the switch, and made me work it. Soon we had a good game going. . . . We were busy with all this for about forty minutes. Perhaps the attention span of infants is not as short as we think. . . .
>
> [Another young child's] patience and concentration are astonishing. . . . She did not get angry or discouraged and worked on it for more than twenty minutes, only stopping when called to lunch. . . .
>
> How much people can learn at any moment depends on how they feel at the moment about the task and their ability to do the task. . . .
>
> Although Danny is only twenty-nine months old he can put these puzzles together with no outside help. . . . The other day . . . [he] couldn't get [one of the pieces] to go right up to the edge. . . . His movements

became more rapid and anxious. Suddenly he turned away from the puzzle, crawled to his blanket, a few feet behind him, grabbed it, stuck his thumb in his mouth and sat down on the floor. (*How Children Learn* by John Holt)

This is, of course, exactly what John Bowlby meant when, in his behavioural science studies, he observed young monkeys who set out to explore but, on finding some frightening object, would scurry back to the mother for safety and protection. Then, having gained succour from her presence, they would set forth again to explore further. Much advice is given on how to help the poor child who feels the need to run into a corner and stick his thumb into his mouth.

But what about the poor teacher who feels exactly the same emotion? I have seen teachers who felt like this. I have been one.

As a young teacher I taught in the heart of Glasgow in Scotland. This was not an easy assignment. The children there were tough, and they tolerated little. However, I had an excellent mentor. The first teacher to whom I was assigned as a young trainee teacher was Anna Thomson. She was five feet nothing, seemed as gentle as a feather, and her classes were always well behaved.

Normally, when we went as trainee teachers to schools to observe trained teachers at work, we were shunted to the back of the class to take notes. This was very interesting for the first ten or twenty minutes and then boredom set in. Imagine my joy when Miss Thomson asked if I would be willing to take the class for a few minutes, as she had some paperwork to take to the office to be signed. I leapt to my feet, and because all trainee teachers had to go to our schools with a lesson ready to teach, just in case the teacher had a minute to watch us perform, I was not only willing, I was prepared. Off she went.

No sooner had she shut the door than the classroom erupted. It was so bad that I had to stand in front of the door to prevent one child from going home. I had only just reinstated peace into the room when Miss Thomson returned. She looked at the class and then looked at me. The scrutiny in these looks was intense. She then turned to the class and told them that she was proud of them and that she had known that they could be relied upon to be good to another teacher. I could not believe my ears. There were some sheepish looks on some faces and some rather apologetic looks on others.

During the morning break I admitted to her that I had not been able to teach anything and that I had barely been able to keep the class under control.

"I knew that," she said. "But you did control them, and you won their respect."

"I don't understand why you were not angry with them."

"Had I been angry with them, they would have resented you, and they would have made you pay. As it is, they think that it was very noble of you not to have told tales on them."

One of the divine qualities of children that I insist on drumming into teachers is their forgiveness. I have seen children behave very badly in a lesson because the teacher failed to maintain their interest, and yet I have seen the same class of children, returning for another lesson with the same teacher one week later, walk into the classroom fairly well behaved and settle down willing to give the teacher another chance. I have seen this happen not once or twice but many, many times. I have seen it happen many times with the same class and the same teacher. Naturally, the amount of time that the class gives to the teacher to produce an interesting lesson shortens each week, until there comes a time when the teacher enters the classroom and is met with instant antagonism. When such a thing happens, I never fail to think how often that class must have suffered and how many of the children in the class have by now become so inculcated with a hatred for teaching, and thereby for learning, that they will never recover. They are doomed to educational failure. That is not fair.

Trust the students, love the students, and they will trust and love you in return. Some students are hard to love. This true, but so are some teachers.

Print our poem on your mind:

Teachers climb these stairs at night
The children stay below
Teachers building fires so bright
That children set aglow
Teaching brings so many joys
To all who would aspire
To help the children, girls or boys
To burn as bright as fire
But please remember when all is done
Did teachers, children, all have fun?

Teaching at nursery level is harder but more rewarding than teaching at higher levels. The children are also more unforgiving. Adult students do not begin to cry or lie down and kick their feet in the air if the lesson becomes boring. Babies can and will. This then makes a nursery school the perfect scenario for teaching teachers how to teach.

At Scottish Academy in Osaka, we run teacher training classes. These classes were started at the request of the head teacher of Tenshi Nursery School in Fukuyama after I had travelled down to Fukuyama several times and taught some EFL lessons to the nursery school children there. Fukuyama is a three-hour drive from Osaka. and so to maximise my time there. I taught three classes back to back with approximately eighty children in each class.

The nursery had a teacher of English as a foreign language, but she thought that as the children had no English ability at all and as they were still too young to read, all lessons had to be taught in Japanese. After watching several of my lessons, she became convinced that that was not the case and decided that she would like to learn how to teach English, in English, to the children. For her, Ethel Ramos, the Ramsay Method was started.

Ethel came to Osaka and studied with us for a week. She was totally dedicated—a wonderful student! At the end of the week, she sat the test for level 1 and passed it. In level 1, the student teacher is expected to teach totally in English without recourse to the native language of the students by constructing a well-balanced lesson with a clear aim, introducing the aim clearly prior to teaching it, showing clear means of consolidating what was taught, and at the end of the lesson testing that the aim had been met.

Ethel was given a lesson plan to fill in each and every time she wanted to teach a lesson. By following this plan, she could ensure that her lessons would be successful. The first part to fill in is the category. By writing in the category (Listening, Pronunciation, Vocabulary, Rhythm, Speaking, Reading, Writing or Grammar), the teacher is made aware of what type of lesson is being taught. It is then easy at the end of the year to add up how many lessons for each category have been taught.

Next, the aim must be written clearly. It need not be long and involved. Simple is best and quickest, because too much time spent in preparation is not good. It must, however, state EXACTLY what the student will know, be able to say or be able to do by the end of the lesson.

Next, the introduction must be written. One word or two here is enough. The students have probably not spoken any English during the previous week, and so the introduction will not only introduce the aim, but it will shower the students with English, refreshing their listening ability. This introduction must be light and entertaining, and above all, no student should be able to see the hook. The aim should be introduced without it being obvious.

If the category is Listening, then an interesting piece of equipment, an unusual poster, or a new game would allow the teacher to talk and explain while the students listened.

If the category is Pronunciation, then the teacher could tell the class a funny story about the some mistake that happened due to bad pronunciation. An example of this is the following true story. A Spanish football team chartered an aeroplane to go to see their home team play internationally. Unfortunately, they booked the aeroplane to go Budapest instead of to Bucharest. Budapest is in Hungary, and Bucharest is in Romania. The students will be introduced to Pronunciation in this manner, and they will never suspect for a moment that they are being introduced to the aim of the lesson. Introducing the aim is akin to showing the students the goal. No one can be expected to score a goal if they cannot see the goal.

The next fifteen minutes is spent in teaching the lesson. In any one-hour lesson, there is only time for fifteen minutes of teaching. If the teacher uses more time than this, the lesson will be faulty, as there will be no time left for consolidating the lesson and testing it. A lesson is well consolidated when the teacher speaks and the student understands. This can be shown by some action or game. A lesson is tested and deemed successful when the student can say correctly whatever it was that was written in the aim as a direct result of something that the teacher says or does.

Now using the Ramsay Method and the lesson plan, both of which are laid out in the next two pages, you can go and teach.

Lesson Plan	
Category:	
Aim:	
15 Minutes	Introduce: (A shower of English)
15 Minutes	Teach:
15 Minutes	Consolidate: (Teacher speaks, student understands)
15 Minutes	Test: (Student speaks)
Items required:	

As shown in this diagram, it is very important to time your lesson well. Only fifteen minutes of an hour-long lesson can be spent in teaching new material; the other three-quarters of an hour must be divided up into introduction, consolidation and testing. Naturally, these times can be pushed and pulled a little. Some classes with a good command of English need less time spent on an introduction, as their ears will soon acclimatise to the foreign language. Never be tempted to cut down on the time spent in consolidation or testing, though. These times are essential. Often, when a lesson goes badly and the teaching aim is not achieved, the incidental learning in the consolidating time is surprising. Of course, the teacher can only know whether the teaching has been successful enough by testing whether it was taught well enough for the target student to be able to use it.

The Ramsay Method

Level 10	The teacher is able to train students to remain in control of what they hear.	
	a)	by showing how to ask appropriate questions
	b)	by showing how to extract clarity from a speaker with a heavy accent
		University
Level 9	The teacher is able to train the students in the grammar of spoken English	
	a)	by showing how to compare it to that of written English
		University
Level 8	The teacher is able to train the students in good penmanship and in the writing of imaginative prose.	
	a)	by introducing the actions necessary for penmanship, in the correct order.
	b)	by showing that the power of English lies in the final part.
		Senior Secondary
Level 7	The teacher is able to train the students to read normal text, text contained within quotation marks, and text written in capital letters.	
	a)	by referring the students back to the spoken English
		Junior secondary
Level 6	The teacher is able to train the students to enunciate standard formatted sentences.	
	a)	by encouraging the students to ask for any items required.
	b)	by encouraging the students to volunteer information
		Junior secondary
Level 5	The teacher is able to train the students to recognize the power carried by a word depending on its position in the sentence	
	a)	by helping the students to alter the rhythm to emphasise on a word
	b)	by helping the students to enunciate numbers clearly and rhythmically
		Primary school
Level 4	The teacher is able to give the students a full understanding of a basic list of 750 words	
	a)	by helping the students to use the vocabulary to understand new words.
		Primary school
Level 3	The teacher is able to help students to eradicate any remnants of their own rhythm.	
	a)	by showing that songs, poems and chants distort the rhythm of a language.
		Primary school
Level 2	The teacher is able to maximize the listening ability of the students by captivating their interest	
	a)	by moving the focus from large muscles to small muscles and then to theory
		Nursery school
Level 1	The teacher is able to teach totally in English without recourse to the native language of the students.	
	a)	by constructing a well balanced lesson with a clear aim
	b)	by introducing the aim clearly prior to teaching it
	c)	by showing clear means of consolidating what was taught
	d)	by testing, at the end of the lesson, that the aim had been met.
		Nursery school

This is the base from which we judge the teaching ability of the teachers. Remember that most teachers teach negatively, but if you teach positively you will enjoy it more, your students will enjoy it more, and they will learn more.

The Golden Rules for Teaching Positively

Do not ask questions.

Every teacher thinks that this is all but impossible. It is not impossible, but it is extremely difficult. Until you can teach without asking questions, try changing the format of the questions so that the sting is removed. "Can anyone tell me . . . " is a good way to start training yourself to stop asking questions. This way, there is no feeling of the finger being pointed at anyone. Of course, there will be those who will never offer an answer to this kind of question. This is no problem. The teacher can safely assume that most of those who did not offer an answer do not know the answer. The same result has been achieved.

The next step in trying to stop yourself asking questions is to practice stating a fact and slowing down to a stop before the end. The students who know the answer cannot refrain from butting in and supplying it. The added bonus in this is that when you do so, if you stand beside a particular student while looking elsewhere, that student knows, as if by magic, that it is he who should supply the answer. Often he will do so. The same student if asked the question directly will, as often as not, fail to supply it. The difference in the two methods is that in the slowing down method, the student is under no pressure, and his mind is free to wander over possible answers. He will be lauded if he finds it but will not be subjected to any abuse from his fellow students or the teacher if he does not.

When asked a direct question, many students who do know the answer but are unsure fill their minds with "hate drivel." *Why did she pick on me? She knows that Joe Soap knows all the answers, but she picks on me. I am not going to answer. See if I care. She can stand there all day if she wants.* With his mind so filled with this "hate drivel," there is no way the student can find the answer. His mind is locked, and worse still, the teacher who does this to him will be in a worse situation next time. This deterioration will build up over time, and the teacher will, in this way, have dug her own grave.

If a student cannot do something, do NOT tell the student.

Tell yourself! Take a note and prepare a good lesson dedicated to that point with that particular child as the target. If the student still does not understand after having a dedicated lesson given to him, tell another teacher and try to find another way to teach the lesson. If, after that, the student still cannot understand or do whatever is necessary, tell the school. The student may have a learning difficulty, such as a hearing problem or poor eyesight that needs correcting.

If a student does something well, tell the student.

Contrary to what should happen, which is to let the student know when he has done well, many teachers seem to think it their duty only to let the student know when he fails to do well. The anomaly of this is that the student in most cases knows very well that he is not doing very well and he often knows why he is not doing very well. He simply does not know how to correct it. Telling a student that he is not doing well and telling him why he is not doing well is more likely to fill his mind with "hate drivel" than to help him find the solution.

If the student does something very well, tell his parents. I have often heard teachers report to parents a student's failings. This never fails to amaze me. Does the teacher think that the parent wants to hear this? No parent wants to listen to such messages. Even if the parent does listen to the message, what can the parent do? One of the most common results of such an attack is that the parent will be angry with the student. This will not endear the student to the teacher and will have put in a huge stumbling block to any future teacher/student rapport. Besides, the parent is most likely not a teacher. You are.

Do your own work. If the student does not pay attention in class, make the lessons more interesting. If the student does not work hard enough, make the lessons more enticing. Whatever you want to accuse the student of doing or not doing is for you yourself to fix.

If the student does something extremely well, tell the world.

Arrange an interschool challenge or something that can show off his prowess. Remember: you are the expert.

Lightning Source UK Ltd.
Milton Keynes UK
UKOW03f2359090514

231405UK00001B/58/P